Streets of Belsize

ISBN 978 0904491 77 7

Chatelain's *View of Hampstead*, 1752.
The foreground shows features of the most northerly part of the huge Belsize estate: Hampstead Green (see Route 1, p 10), Pond Street (Route 9) and the fields stretching up to Hampstead Heath and Parliament Hill (Route 10). Some houses in the middle distance are still standing.

Streets of Belsize

A survey of streets,
buildings & former residents
in a part of Camden

Second edition newly revised by Christopher Wade
Edited by F Peter Woodford
Designed by Ivor Kamlish

Diagram of the walks

For detailed maps see
pages 10, 30, 45 and 64

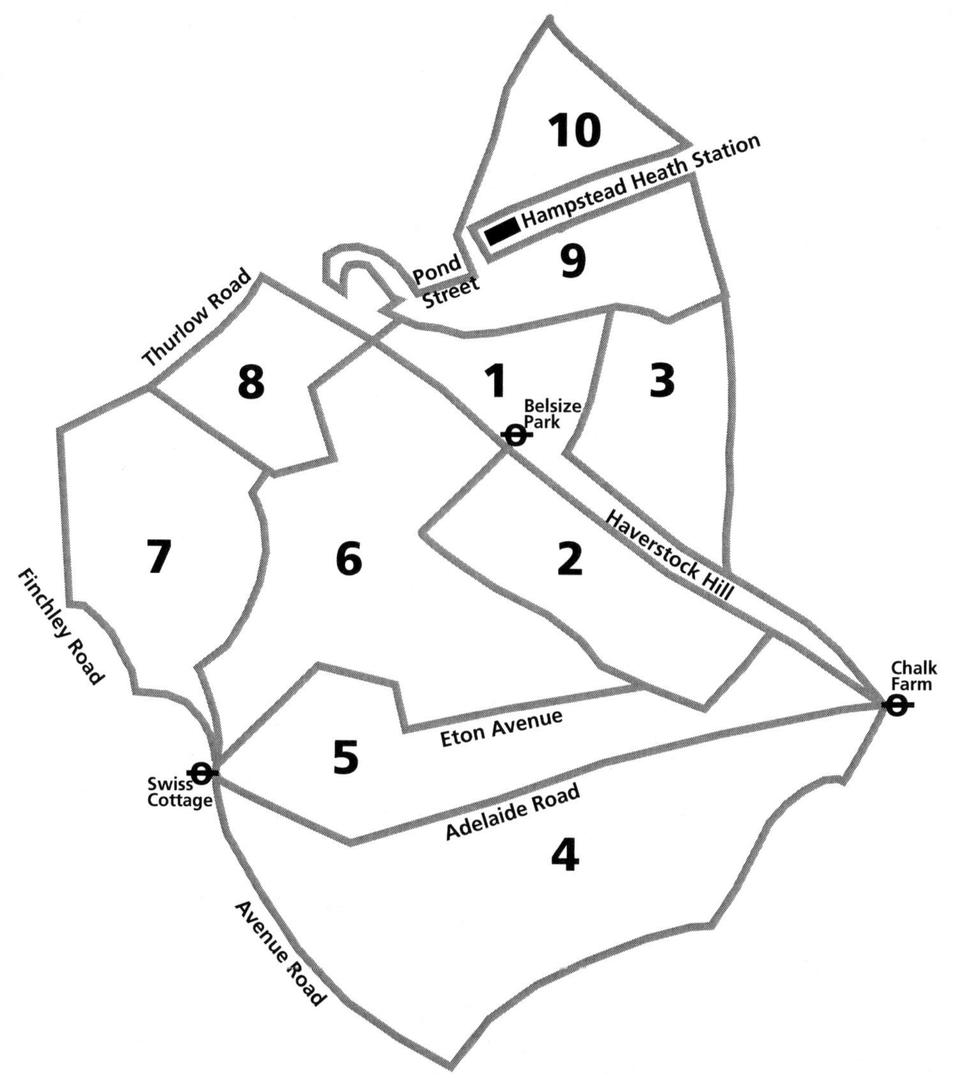

Contents

List of maps and illustrations

Sketch maps

Frontispiece

Illustrations

Historical overview

1 Belsize House, the 18th-century version

Belsize means 'beautifully situated'. Originally Bel Assis in French, the name is cheerfully adapted by English cartographers into Belsyse (Norden 1593), Bellsize (Ogilby 1672) and all possible other versions until the early eighteenth century (e.g. Milward 1702), when the current spelling began to find favour. An estate within the manor of Hampstead, Belsize's existence was not recorded until 1317, when Sir Roger le Brabazon left this 'messuage and fifty-seven acres of land in Hampstede' to Westminster Abbey. Sir Roger was Lord Chief Justice to Edward II, and the first of Belsize's absentee landlords. He left all this land to the monks of Westminster in return for masses to be said for his soul and for that of the Earl of Lancaster (cf. Lancaster Grove, p 51).

According to F M L Thompson in his *Hampstead, Building a Borough*, the first Belsize House was probably erected in 1496, with the use of 400,000 bricks from a brickfield north of Belsize Lane. The resultant excavated area is now occupied by the fenced-off enclosure of eight houses, Village Close. The first Belsize

House was rebuilt about 1663 and again sometime after 1745 **[1]**. In 1540, after his dissolution of the monasteries, Henry VIII gave the estate to the new bishopric of Westminster, but it reverted to the Dean and Chapter of Westminster after the bishopric expired in 1550. The property was leased to Armigell Waad for the annual rent of £19 2s 10d and ten loads each of hay and oats. Waad has been wildly called by one historian 'the English Columbus' because he was among the first of his countrymen to discover America. Hakluyt records only that Waad went on the 1536 expedition to Newfoundland, during which "they suffered from famine to such a degree that the ship's company began to devour one another". More certainly, Waad was a Clerk of the Council to Henry VIII and Edward VI, and he retired to Belsize House, where he died in 1567. He was buried in Hampstead Parish Church "under a fair monument of alabaster", but this has disappeared. Armigell's son William succeeded him not only as owner of the estate but eventually as a Clerk to the Council under Elizabeth and James I, who knighted him. In a letter dated August 1603 to his friend Robert Cecil, Sir William complained that the Belsize area was being invaded by Londoners escaping from the plague epidemic in the city. "Divers come out of the town", he wrote, "and dy under Hedges in the feilds...whereof we have experience weekeley here at Hampsted." He recommended in vain that these refugees be fined. During the Civil War, Sir William's widow mortgaged the Belsize estate to raise money for the royalist cause, but the mortgagee being a Roundhead, she lost the house when the king lost the war.

At the Restoration, the lease went to Colonel Daniel O'Neill, Gentleman of the Bedchamber to Charles II and third husband of the adventurous Catherine, Lady Stanhope and Countess of Chesterfield. He rebuilt Belsize House in 1663 but the following year, as Charles II noted, "poor O'Neill died of an ulcer in the guts". His stepson, Lord Wotton, inherited and improved the property, probably using the younger of the Tradescant family (now mostly remembered by the eponymous house plant) to develop the gardens. Samuel Pepys visited Lord Wotton on 17 August 1668, and recorded in his diary that the gardens were "too good for the house... the most noble that ever I saw, and brave orange and lemon trees". A decade later, however, another diarist, John Evelyn, found the gardens ill-kept and the soil "a cold weeping clay".

After Lord Wotton's death in 1683, Belsize passed to his half-brother Philip, second Earl of Chesterfield, but he never lived there and from about 1704 he sub-let the property on a series of life-leases. The first lessee was an enterprising character called Charles Povey. "A man of scheming and speculative turn", Povey had already achieved some fame as a pamphleteer and as the proprietor of a halfpenny postal service. This latter project being illegal, he was fined £100. He now opened Belsize House and gardens to the public. This included a wed-wine-and-dine scheme whereby you could be married in the private chapel (Sion Chapel) for five shillings, as long as your wedding feast was kept in the gardens. Among other entertainments offered was the hunting of wild deer in the park, with a sixpenny lottery for a share of the venison. In 1720, Povey sub-let again to a wily Welshman called Howell, self-styled 'His Excellency the Welsh Ambassador'. At a time when Hampstead Spa in Well Walk was losing favour, Belsize rose to the height of its fame as Pleasure Gardens, a forerunner of Ranelagh and Vauxhall – and Alexandra Palace. Open from 6am to 8pm, it offered music, dancing, gambling, deer-hunting (Thursdays and Saturdays), duck-hunting, horse-racing, footman-racing and plenty of secluded arbours for other unmentionable pleasures. The management also provided gamblers and other guests with a get-you-home protection service. "There will be twelve stout fellows, completely armed, to patrol between London and Belsize."

In 1721, the Prince and Princess of Wales dined at the house "and at their departure were very liberal to the servants". The following year "the appearance of nobility and gentry at Belsize was so great that they reckoned between three and four hundred coaches". Belsize flourished fitfully for another twenty years or so but, as Barratt says, it became "over-boisterous and lost its manners, polite society declined to be drawn by its coarse attractions". He also quotes some of the printable parts of the satirical ballad of Belsize House, such as:

> Sodom of old was a more righteous
> Place;
> For angels hence four righteous Souls
> could call;
> But at Belsize, by Heav'n! there's none
> at all…

What with this riotous behaviour and the traffic jams in Belsize Avenue, the local residents had the place closed down by the magistrates, just as they had clamped down on the Well Walk spa. "The Wicked Part at length broke in", wrote Daniel Defoe about Belsize House in 1724. "No British Government could be supposed to bear long with the Liberties taken."

In 1807, an Act of Parliament empowered the Chesterfield family, the current lessees, to sell the Belsize Estate of 234 acres, and it was bought by a syndicate of four local men. Belsize House was pulled down in 1853, and *The Illustrated London News* of the time referred to the "leasing of the noble park to such Londoners as may wish to retire from the smoke and bustle of the town to that pleasant airy suburb rendered classical by the famous spirits by whom it has been inhabited during the last two centuries". The list of 'spirits' included Steele, Keats and Akenside, all of whom are now commemorated by local street names. The first streets were laid out in the 1850s, and most of the main thoroughfares were built up by 1866. Westminster Abbey ended its main connection with the Belsize Estate in 1887, largely passing its interests to the Church Commissioners. By 1900, Belsize Park was much as it appears today.

The history of the other two main estates covered by this survey is mainly agricultural. South of Belsize, the Eton College estate was originally Chalcots (later Chalk Farm), for long the property of St James' Leper Hospital at Westminster, but granted to Eton College by its founder Henry VI in 1449. The estate kept its rural look until soon after Nash laid out Regent's Park in the 1820s, when developers began to look to adjacent areas on which to build desirable residences.

In 1995 the College decided to pull out of the Chalcots Estate and sold over 1000 of its residential properties for little more than £4 million. The new landlords of the 1300 flats and 140 houses, a consortium of Compco and Southend Property Holdings, became the biggest freeholders in Hampstead.

To the east of Belsize, across Haverstock Hill – the main artery running down from Hampstead to London – a small but ambitious development of the 1860s was named St John's Park, but although the handsome houses and streets remain, the name never took off like Belsize Park or St John's Wood, and has been virtually forgotten. Here, as in many other parts of Belsize Park, the builders Batterbury & Huxley were responsible for many of the tall red-brick houses and villas.

To the north and west of Belsize lay the Maryon Wilson estate, land belonging to the Lords of the Manor of Hampstead; the parts of their estate covered by this book were known as Belsize Farm, Manor Farm, or the Conduit Fields (around Shepherd's Well). Because of legal complications, the family were not able to sell off their land to the many eager speculators until the 1870s, when Fitzjohn's Avenue and its prestigious surroundings were successfully built. Leigh Hunt's "dear gentle hill, with tresses green and bright" has mostly disappeared, but the area now known as Belsize Park provides an elegant, variegated frill to Hampstead, "a village revelling in varieties".

Route 1

Down Haverstock Hill

From Hampstead Green
to the former "Load of Hay"
For map see below

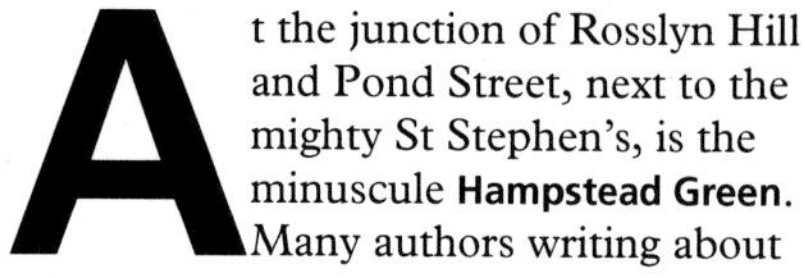

At the junction of Rosslyn Hill and Pond Street, next to the mighty St Stephen's, is the minuscule **Hampstead Green**. Many authors writing about Hampstead at the end of the 19th century say that they can remember it when it really was a green. Anna Maxwell described it as a "wide slope of grass, shaded by very tall trees, and reaching down to a round, railed-

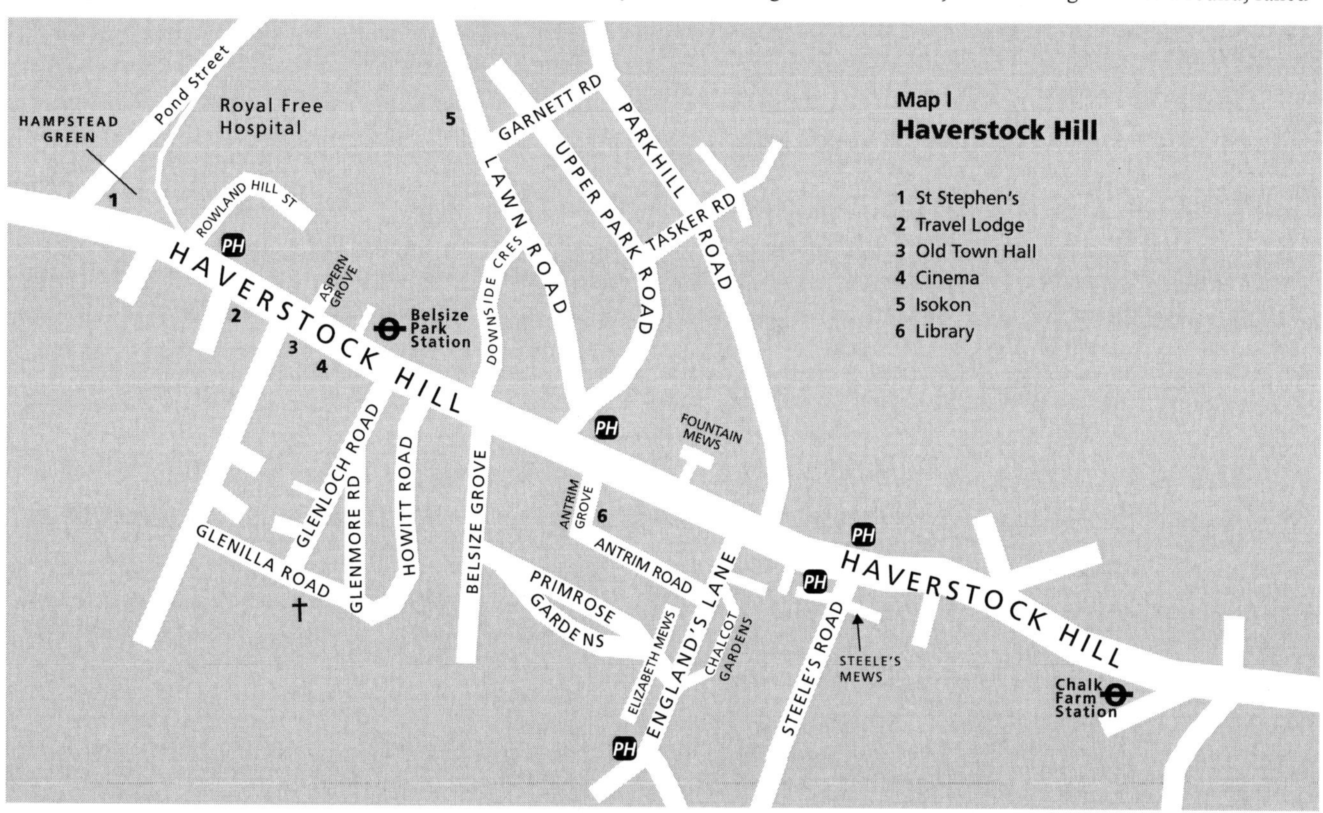

in pool at the bottom of Pond Street".

Standing along the south-eastern edge of the green were several Georgian houses, which sheltered from the 1850s onwards some of the nationally better-known inhabitants of Hampstead. In the most southern house, Bartrams, lived Lord Sidney Godolphin Osborne, the philanthropist. Next came Bartram House, the residence of Sir Rowland Hill. This man, best known today as the originator of the Penny Post, lived there for thirty years until his death in 1879. (Bartram is one of Belsize's oldest names, belonging to a family who owned property here in the 13th century.) Sir Rowland was the leader of the unsuccessful fight to prevent the building of a smallpox hospital in the neighbourhood. The Metropolitan Asylums Board had bought some eight acres of the adjoining land, the Bartrams estate, for the North Western Fever Hospital, which opened in 1870, and in 1883 Hill's son sold Bartram House also to the Board, who used it for a nurses' home. The house was demolished in 1902 and the new 50-bed Hampstead General Hospital was opened on the site in 1905. This was itself included in the Royal Free group in 1948, and was demolished in 1975, since when the site of Hill's house has been used as a car park for the new hospital.

The north-west wall of the underground car park carries a brown plaque commemorating Hill's residence, as does the dull little cul-de-sac nearby, **ROWLAND HILL STREET**, which leads to the Royal Free School of Medicine. Above the car park is a small garden dedicated to Dr Heath Strange, the benefactor and founder of the Hampstead General Hospital. Displayed here are the original façade lettering and the foundation stone of the old hospital, laid by HRH Princess Christian of Schleswig-Holstein in 1902. On the south side of Rowland Hill Street is **Bartrams Hostel**, built in 1955-57, on the site of the convent and orphanage established in 1867 by the Sisters of Providence and of the Immaculate Conception: this was destroyed in an air raid in 1940. As well as a convent, the new building is now an international and interdenominational hostel for students. The dramatic sculpture of the Mater Ecclesiae on the front of the building is by Michael Werner (Baron Michael Werner von Alvensleben, 1912-89). The gaunt red-brick block rising behind the hostel is part of the **Rosary Roman Catholic Primary School** on Haverstock Hill. It was built in 1887 by C G Wray as additional accommodation for the convent's private boarding school.

Another important house which disappeared from the green early last century was Tensleys. Reputedly the lodgings in the 1830s of the French diplomat Talleyrand, this was the home in the 1850s of Francis Palgrave, compiler of *The Golden Treasury*, and later of S S Teulon, the maverick architect of **St Stephen's Church**. For this weighty church, built in 1869-73 on a patch of manorial waste, Teulon used purple-red Dunstable brick, with bands of rag and granite – known to some as his 'streaky bacon style', but to others as neo-Gothic with 'strong French connections'. One critic called it "Half a house of God, Half a Castle on the Rhine": Pevsner in 1952 found it "insensitive and ham-fisted", but the Pevsner edition of 1998 (revised by Bridget Cherry) admitted that "appreciation had grown of this forceful and original architect". Ruskin hailed it as "the finest specimen of brick-building in all the land", and many a climber of Haverstock Hill has acclaimed its tower as a final punctuation mark. St Stephen's originally seated 1,250, but it suffered neglect and some subsidence. More serious cracks appeared in 1969, as the foundations of the new hospital were excavated, and the church was officially closed in 1977. As alternative uses for this remarkable building were endlessly debated (they included a riding stable and a Japanese restaurant), the church remained squatted and despoiled, unlovely and apparently unloved, except by the pigeons. But in 1999 the St Stephen's Restoration and Preservation Trust was founded to restore and convert the church "for purposes of education and for the benefit of the community of Hampstead". Since then, several million pounds have been raised, much helped by the Heritage Lottery Fund and much by the efforts of the

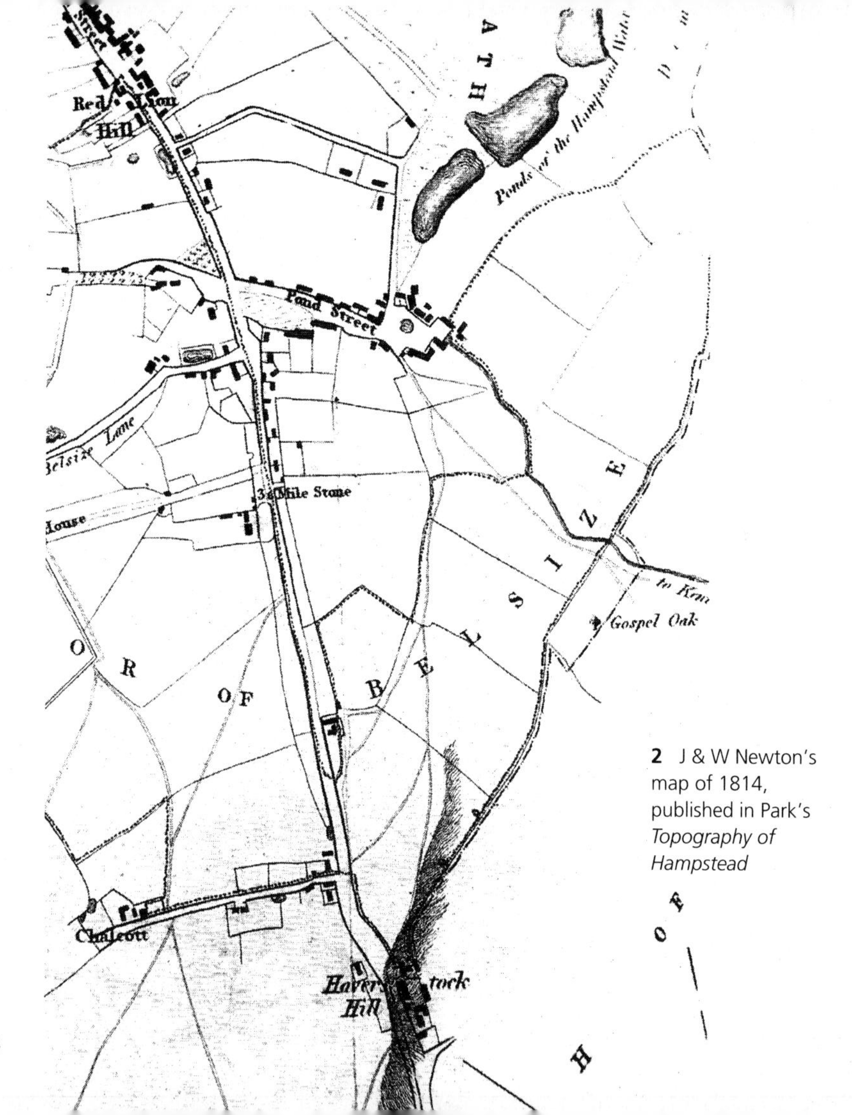

2 J & W Newton's map of 1814, published in Park's *Topography of Hampstead*

adjoining Hampstead Nursery School (led by architect Michael Taylor). The building is to reopen in March 2009.

On the west side of the present green is the **wooden refreshment hut**, originally a cabmen's shelter, which has a splendid mosaic floor (by John Cooper), inscribed 'The Wharrie Shelter, April 1935'. Mary Wharrie was the daughter of Hampstead's first mayor, Sir Henry Harben, and 1935 was the year she was given, in return for her many local benefactions, the Freedom of the Borough.

HAVERSTOCK HILL is presumed to be the 'Foxhangra' mentioned in the 10th-century records of Hampstead, but it is not seen on a map until John Norden's Middlesex of 1593. The name was first mentioned in Rocque's map of 1745, where it was used to indicate the definite and very steep hill by Steele's Cottage and the Load of Hay (p 17). It seems to have been connected with the area of the hill **[2]** rather than with the roadway itself, which was then, and for long afterwards, known as Hampstead Hill or the London Road, according to one's location. One theory suggests that the name is derived from the Latin *averia*, meaning a pasture. A second and more likely proposal is that it is an Anglo-Saxon word formed from *haver*, meaning oats (as in Haverhill) and stock, a place. Oats were certainly grown in this area, as they constituted part of the Belsize estate's rent to Westminster Abbey in the 16th century.

No other Haverstock exists today, but until the 18th century the village of Stock, east of Ingatestone in Essex, was called by that name. Only gradually did the name come to refer to the roadway from Belsize Lane to Chalk Farm. It was finally established as the official Post Office address for the whole of its present length in 1876, when the present numbering system was given.

From the Chalk Farm toll-gate (removed in 1864), cottages, and then houses and villas, crept up the hill as London grew beyond Regent's Park and Camden Town. They engulfed the settlement round Steele's Cottage and continued up until they met the spread of Hampstead coming down.

At the top of Haverstock Hill, the collection of buildings that includes **The George** public house constituted a group known as Bellevue. The tavern, first mentioned in the licensing records of 1715, was noted for its tea gardens and also served as a post office. An early name for the pub was the Great Tree, being next to the famous Hollow Elm (see *CHR*19 pp4-6) and in 1999 it shamefully (but briefly) became The Rat and Parrot. By the 1860s postal business had been transferred to **No.240**, at the other end of this highly decorated terrace, which also included Hampstead's first fire station, opened in 1869.

On the other side of the road, between Belsize Lane and Ornan Road, stood Ivy Bank, built in 1804 at the eastern end of George Todd's estate (**[15]**, p 47). It was the home until 1833 of the Willoughby family, who left their name on Willoughby Road, much further up the hill into Hampstead. Divided in two and renamed Elm House and Belsize Lodge, the mansion was demolished and rebuilt as a flamboyant Victorian villa under its original name around 1875. In 1893 the tycoon Alfred Ridley Bax used it as his headquarters while he was developing Ornan Road. His sons, (Sir) Arnold and Clifford, distinguished themselves in music and drama respectively. Now the landscape is dominated by the **Premier Travel Lodge**, formerly the Post House Hotel, which opened in 1970. Vandervell Bros Ltd. had their 'Motor Car Garage' on this Haverstock Hill frontage from the early 1930s, and the hotel's restaurant had as its predecessor on the site in 1932 the Hot Dog Limited Refreshment Rooms.

Below Belsize Avenue, the old **Hampstead Town Hall** was built in 1877-78 to designs by H E Kendall and Frederick Mew (father of Charlotte Mew, the Bloomsbury poet). The red-brick and stone Italianate building, with its towering belvedere, was much admired at the time, but was derided by Pevsner in the 1950s as "crushingly mean, a disgrace to so prosperous and artistic a borough". The building was certainly in mean condition by 1994, when Camden Council closed it down and considered selling it. But the Town Hall was then declared a Listed Building and through the efforts of local community activists its fortunes were improved by a restoration project, The Hamden Trust, launched by The Friends of Hampstead Town Hall, Interchange Studios and the Council. The refurbished building was opened by HRH the Prince of Wales in June 2000. Users of the new Town Hall include various small enterprises and charities, such as the University of the Third Age. A large part of the building is devoted to Interchange Studios, which provides specialist facilities for young people and the disabled, and includes the successful WAC Performing Arts and Media College. The halls are once again available to the local community for hire. The old Town Hall can just be made out in Clausen's 1881 painting **[3]** which looks up the hill from a point outside what is now Daunt's Belsize bookshop or what would be then the fence of Hillfield.

The land between Belsize Avenue and Belsize Grove used to contain two large estates, Hillfield and Woodlands, both occupied by members of the Woodd family. Basil George Woodd had come to Hampstead in 1826 and was a successful wine merchant: he was known as the 'father of the London wine trade'. According to Baines, he was descended from the royal houses of both England and France (though rather remotely), and numbered amongst many other famous ancestors both John Hampden and Captain Basil Woodd to whom, says Baines, Charles I handed his Garter Star on the morning of his execution.

This diversity of outlook in his ancestry perhaps helped to produce in Basil George his benevolent and public-spirited attitude, inherited by his sons, two of whom were also local celebrities. He lived first on Hampstead Green, and then from 1841 at Hillfield, where he died in 1872, aged 91. His successor, who sold off small parts of the estate to Hampstead Vestry and large plots to developers, was Charles Paine,

3 *Spring Morning, Haverstock Hill* (Sir George Clausen, 1881) showing a glimpse of St Stephen's behind the Rosary School on the right (Courtesy Bury Art Gallery)

whose second name was Cleverly: he died at Hillfield in 1934. The 14-acre Hillfield estate took its shape and name from the Hill Field, shown on the 1679 map of Belsize's rural acres. It has now passed the name on to **Hillfield Mansions**, the 1930s flats above the shops, which neatly embrace a branch of **The Everyman**, a bijou cinema on the site of a previous cinema, the Screen on the Hill. Standing outside the cinema, note the good view of St Paul's Cathedral.

Next down the hill, Woodlands (or Wooddlands?) must have appeared less impressive from the road, but as a compensation had large grounds at the back. This wooded area is also shown on the 1679 map. The house was built in the mid-1860s by Basil George's second son, R B Woodd, who had formerly lived down the hill in Devonshire Place. The third son, C H L Woodd, lived just up the road at Rosslyn House (p 65).

Across the road, the ground between the Rosary School and Upper Park Road formerly accommodated two estates – Bartram Park (not to be confused with Bartrams) and Haverstock Lodge. With the advent of the fever hospital (p 11), Bartram Park became less desirable as a private residence and was turned into a girls' industrial home, called Tre Wint. The grounds had been somewhat blighted by the construction of two tunnels for the main Midland Railway out of St Pancras, which pass below Haverstock Hill by **No.214** (southern tunnel, 1865-67) and **No.228** (northern, 1881-84). Its brick-built circular ventilation shafts may be seen behind **Nos.208** and **224** Haverstock Hill.

In the 1890s a portion of the nine-acre Bartram estate was leased from the railway company by John Russell for his nursery garden, and other parts were laid out as tennis courts. After WWII the main area became Russell's Sports Ground, and in 1972 the whole estate was bought by Camden Council. The new housing development, costing some £14 million, was completed in the 1990s and includes 184 homes, a woodland nature reserve, a new footpath to Lawn Road, and the long-established **Globe Lawn Tennis Club**. A modern, Lego-like skeletal arch, which leads to this colourful and spacious estate, designed by Camden's own architects, carries the inexplicable label **ASPERN GROVE**. Other roads are called **WOODLAND WALK** and **RUSSELL PLACE**. Several buildings have delightful mosaics made by Rise Phoenix in 2003/4. The nature reserve, now known as Belsize Wood, has become an attractive wild-life haven.

Resistance heroine Odette Churchill, GC, lived at **No.216 Haverstock Hill** for a short time in 1955; soon afterwards the house became a restaurant. Lower down, a series of cafés and restaurants have happily spread onto the wider pavements, weather permitting, and given this stretch of Haverstock Hill a continental flavour. Below is **Belsize Park Tube Station**, which was opened in 1907 as part of the Charing Cross, Euston and Hampstead Railway. The distinctive station exteriors for this line, with their oxblood red tiles, were all designed by Leslie Green, but much of this structure has been altered.

Belsize Park station became a popular air raid shelter in the last war, and its sleeping shelterers were the inspiration for Henry Moore's famous series of sketches: he was then living in Parkhill Road (p 27). "One evening we returned home by Underground to Belsize Park," he wrote. "I had never seen so many reclining figures, and even the train tunnels seemed to be like the holes in my sculptures." Lesser known is the extra Deep Shelter constructed under the Tube platforms here (and at nine other Tube stations). The shelter stretches along twin tunnels, bisected horizontally, for over a quarter of a mile – from a point below the old Haverstock Arms (p 16) to below the Royal Free. Visible from the surface are the massive access shafts, topped with bomb- and gas-proof steel and concrete caps, which stand next to Downside Crescent (p 23) and **Allingham Court** (named after Helen and William Allingham, see p 69). The Deep Shelter belongs to the Ministry of Defence and still has its 9,000 steel bunk beds in place. These make useful storage racks for an archives security firm, which now leases the 5,500 ft of tunnel.

Further down the hill, beyond Downside Crescent, the four pairs of semi-detached houses, **Nos.156-170**, were built as part of the Haverstock Lodge estate, which was developed by William Lund in the early 1860s. Nos.156-162 were originally named Ormesby, Stanley, Thanet and Rickham Houses. Nos.164-170 were known as 1-4 Oak Villas before systematic numbering by the Post Office in 1876. The original resident of Stanley House (No.160) was Major-General T J Nuttall, who retired there after his 50th Native Indian Regiment mutinied. A later resident here in 1940 was the critic and poet (Sir) William Empson, who during WWII was the editor of the BBC Chinese Service. The garage next to No.164 has recently been developed into a space-age maisonette called **Garden House**.

On the west side of Haverstock Hill, at the corner of Belsize Grove, stood Bedford Lodge, home of John Maple, owner of the furniture store. (His monument in Highgate Cemetery is shaped like a bed.) In an adjoining house, then called No.5 Devonshire Place, lived the railway engineer Robert Stephenson from 1836 to 1842. His wife, Frances, died here and was buried in Hampstead churchyard. Almost all the old villas below Belsize Grove on this side of the hill have been replaced with blocks of flats. The latest and least blockish are **Nos.143-145**, which are partly on the site of the Elizabeth Garrett Anderson Maternity Home. The bays, balconies and porticoes of the new building were designedly similar to those of the old one.

After **Romney Court**, presumably commemorating the painter's residence in Holly Bush Hill in the heart of Hampstead, comes one of the few original terraces remaining on the west side of the road, **Nos.129-133**. A Buddhist monastery was once based here, and when No.131 was put up for sale in 1977 it was said to include a Buddhist temple and three meditation cells in the garden. This trio of stock-brick houses of 1820 are among the few Listed Buildings in the street. Among the flat-lands to the south, **No.119** was the home and studio for many years of the popular artist Sydney Arrobus (1901-90).

Outside the **Havers** restaurant across the road there is a Listed telephone kiosk, one of Sir Giles Gilbert Scott's beloved designs c.1927. The previous pub's eye-catching mural was completed by John Murray in 1984 and achieved fame in a book of the best pub-signs in the land. It has now vanished. To the south is **Crown Cottage, 150A**, where, it is said (without proof) that Charles II stayed the night while his horse was shod. Then comes handsome **Crown Lodge, No.148**, dating from the early 19th century, one of the oldest surviving houses in Belsize Park. It has a Grecian decorated front, a battlemented back and a crenellated fence. The house and the garden wall are Listed.

A bold piece of in-filling in 1970 was the insertion of two flats at **Nos.142-144**. The Studio on the ground floor of No.144 was built for James Gardner, the artist responsible for the QE2 Upper Deck, and a specialist in museum interiors. The aluminium and glass first floor contrasts with the solid Victorian block, **Nos.136-140**, built around 1856 as Nos.1-3 Elm Villas. No.140 was for many years the home of the artist Stephen Bone, who died here in 1959, and of his artist wife Mary Adshead. No.138 was occupied in 1859 by the civil engineer Alfred Dickens, younger brother of Charles Dickens, who is buried in Highgate Cemetery.

The columned entrance below **No.128** leads to an elegant new enclave, **Fountain Mews**. This was built in 1994 on a derelict salt store by the Community Housing Association and, among other accommodation, included nine one-bedroom flats for the homeless. **Nos.104-116**, the Victorian houses on both sides of the junction with Parkhill Road, were earmarked for demolition in the Council's Borough Plan of 1974, but after protests that they were sound stock, familiar landmarks, and made a pleasant endstop to England's Lane, they were happily saved and refurbished by the Belpark Housing Cooperative in 1985. Also notable is the coach house of **No.96**, dated (1890), initialled GM (George Munro) and cartouched.

Where the hill begins to dip sharply was the original little settlement of Haverstock Hill. Until about the 1850s, the only house on the western side was the cottage which had been the home in 1712 of the writer Sir Richard Steele, and before him of the poet Sir Charles Sedley, who came there to die in poverty in 1702. For Steele it was a convenient spot, far enough from urban life to discourage his creditors from pursuing him, and near enough to Hampstead to enable him to attend the meetings of the Kit Cat Club in the Upper Flask (see *The Streets of Hampstead*). The cottage, later converted into two dwellings, was a picturesque landmark until it was pulled down in 1867 to make way for Steele's Road. Steele has, nevertheless, been commemorated to a far greater extent than most Hampstead notables. Apart from the road name, there is the **Sir Richard Steele** public house, **Steele's Studios**, and the shopping terraces, once known jointly as Steele's Terrace. In front of these shops is the old milestone marking 'four miles from the Post Office' in St Martin le Grand.

Among the Studios' distinguished artists, C R W Nevinson stands out for his WWI pictures and other work in Vorticist style, viewable at Tate Britain and the Imperial War Museum. He was born in Hampstead, the son of H W Nevinson (p 24) and grandson of Basil Woodd (p 13), and died at Steele's Studios in 1946. A painting by him of Haverstock Hill is in the Hampstead Museum at Burgh House. Another long-term resident at the Studios, also a war artist, was Edmond Kapp, who died here in 1978: he was famed especially for his portrait drawings. The Studios were built by Thomas Batterbury in 1872.

4 *Sir Richard Steele's Cottage, Hampstead* by John Constable, 1832. Looking south to St Paul's, the cottage is on the right, the Load of Hay tavern on the left

Steele's Cottage and its fine view over London and St Paul's appeared in many prints and paintings, notably in one by Constable in 1832 **[4]**. Among the houses often seen in these pictures are the tall Georgian buildings, **Nos.82-84**, the terrace below the public house. No.84 and all buildings down the hill to Prince of Wales Road were originally in St Pancras, but were transferred to Hampstead in 1900.

The tavern now known as **The Hill** was formerly the famous Load of Hay, mentioned in licensing records from 1721. At some time before that it was named the Cart and Horses, and more recently the Noble Art because of a gymnasium at the back (said to have been favoured by boxers Henry Cooper and Muhammad Ali). The pub still bears its proper name The Load of Hay and its building date – 1864 – on its parapet and is Listed for its 'good metalwork' and other features. In his *Tales of a Traveller*, Washington Irving, who stayed at Steele's Cottage in 1824, described the Irish haymakers and the drovers and teamsters to whom this country pub was the 'local'. This was not its only function by any means. For some time it boasted a fashionable tea-garden and, more importantly, it was a standard stop for coaches on their way up and down the hill.

The Load of Hay's most famous landlord, Joe Davis **[5]**, was known as 'The Host of Haverstock Hill' in the late 18th century, and seems to have been one of his own best customers. A huge man, his drunken antics and eccentrically splendid clothes provided a great attraction. His death was characteristic. One evening in 1806, he threw himself down on the bar as usual. No one took any more notice than on any other evening, and so he lay there undisturbed until bedtime, when he was found to be dead.

The eastern side of the lower part of Haverstock Hill down to Chalk Farm station is fully covered in *Streets of Gospel Oak and West Kentish Town*. On the other, western, side, the old Nos.1-59 were replaced by large blocks of flats from the end of the 1930s (see Eton College Road, p 44). No.53 was one of the many Hampstead homes of artist Mark Gertler, who is well represented in Tate Britain and elsewhere. Below the back gate of Eton Hall, a **boundary stone** points out that old Hampstead's parish boundary ran down the middle of the road. As with most of Hampstead's boundary lines, this one had remained unchanged for 1000 years or more.

5 *Joe Davis*,
landlord of the Load of Hay,
1804 drawing

Route 2

West of Haverstock Hill

From Glenloch Road to Steele's Road

For map see p 10

A group of roads on the west of Haverstock Hill, just south of the old Town Hall (p 13), was developed from 1900 onwards on the grounds of two gentlemen's residences, Hillfield and Woodlands (pp 13, 14). The four roads, which are united by a visual touch – octagonal turrets at the top of Glenloch and Howitt Roads, and another at the bottom of Glenmore – are all small-scale, coming after the building slump of the 1890s and away from the mighty mansions of classical Belsize.

We begin by examining the terraced family houses of **GLENLOCH ROAD** and **GLENMORE ROAD**, which show a wide variety of Edwardian decorative features – tiled entrances, stained glass, art-nouveau fretwork and dados, and assorted bay windows. Glenmore Road is notably rich in stained-glass doors, including **Nos.8,10,15** and **16**, and in well-preserved pargetting panels, for example **No.55**. Four successive blocks of flats filled the wedge-shaped junction of the two roads in the 1930s, necessitating the removal of some tall trees (with resident owls) and a valued open space. **Wimborne Mansions** is named after its builder, Simon Wimborne of Heath Street.

The only other break in the Edwardian style is the Tudorised gateway next to **No.40** Glenloch Road, which leads to Tudor Close (p 55). Note the elegant fish-scale roof-tiles hereabouts. The most recent addition to Glenloch Road is **Tagore House**, built on the former Odeon Cinema car park and named after the Indian poet who lived briefly in the Vale of Health. Lovers of the drama will like to know that the playwright Alan Ayckbourn was born at **No.32** Glenloch, which in 1939 was the Westridge Nursing Home, and that the actor Robert Powell became a father at **No.43** Glenmore in 1977. Graham Hill, the racing driver, lived at **No.63** Glenmore after WWII, and his son Damon, also a Formula One World Champion, was born there in 1960.

The street names in this area derive from the Glenloch Investment Company, which developed them. They seem straightforwardly fanciful, customer-attracting names, with a Scottish lilt, until one comes to **GLENILLA ROAD**, which seems to go beyond mere fancy. It was the first road of the four to be laid out, and its construction accounts for the disappearance of No.36 Belsize Park Gardens. At **No.32** is the Church of the Christian Community, built in 1948 on the site of a tennis court. The architect, Kenneth Bayes, made the most of the prefabricated materials available, and a lady woodworker of the congregation carved the interesting doorway "inspired by the works of Rudolf Steiner". Professor Joel Hurstfield, the distinguished historian of Tudor times, was long resident at **No.7** and died there in 1980.

The south-west side of this road has always been largely occupied by studios, backing on to the original boundary of the Belsize Estate. The Dutch-style gables of **No.2 Belsize Studios**, notable for its garden entrance, echo similar gables in Belsize Avenue. On the other side of the road, **Nos.17&19** are a homely pair of 1920s cottages, with an unusual hexagonal plaque. In the 1930s No.19 was owned by H G Wells's elder son George, an eminent professor of zoology.

Glenilla Road ends in **HOWITT ROAD**; turn left up the hill. It was named after the popular writer William Howitt, author of *The Northern Heights of London* (1869); he and his literary wife Mary were residents of Highgate but also lovers of Hampstead. As the blue plaque shows, **No.9** was the home from 1916-25 of Ramsay MacDonald, the first Labour Prime Minister. Here he formed his first Cabinet before moving to Downing Street; he later climbed the hill to a grander house in Frognal. The elaborate brickwork, terracotta and turrets of **Nos.20-26** contrast with the necessarily utilitarian style of **Nos.31-35**, rebuilt after bombing in WWII.

Regain Haverstock Hill and take the next turning right, south of the Glens group, into **BELSIZE GROVE**. On the left corner, the Elizabeth Garrett Anderson Maternity Home has been replaced by town houses, **Nos.40-48**. The fine adjoining terrace, **Nos.26-38**, once known as Haverstock Terrace, was built in 1825-26 by George Crane, and then stood alone in "a short road with a gate at the end and fields beyond". The central house with its head of Hope (now in fibreglass) in the pediment and spreading catalpa tree in the front garden is particularly handsome. F W Watts (1800-62), the landscape artist much influenced by Constable, lived in No.38. A century later, another artist, John Farleigh, noted for his wood engravings, lived at No.36. The arts critic and broadcaster Jack Lambert died at No.30 in 1986. The architect Richard Rogers, 'the high priest of hi-tech', lived at **No.18** in the 1970s and 1980s, while designing the Lloyds Building. **No. 22** has miraculously kept its original porch, railings and (part) boot scraper.

On the right, the 1930s flats, **Holmefield Court** and **Gilling Court**, were named respectively after Home Field, which appears on the manor map of 1762, and Gilling Lodge, shown on an 1862 map. Then come examples of the old porticoed style Victorian houses, **Nos.5-11**. They are characteristic of all this part of Belsize Park, being described by Simon Jenkins in his *Companion Guide to Outer London* as "the ramparts of Italianate Belsize Park". The actress Dame Peggy Ashcroft (1907-81) lived at Nos.9&11 in the 1980s. Finally, after **Straffan Lodge**, a block of flats built in 1969, we observe one of the pioneers of purpose-built flats for the rich in London, **Manor Mansions** (1884). The apartments are of generous proportions – especially on the first floor, which retains the style of a *piano nobile*.

The road now called **PRIMROSE GARDENS**, which leads off between the Nos.18 and 22 mentioned above, was laid out across the grounds of the original Hampstead Cricket Club by 1862 and named Stanley Gardens, after one of the Deans of Westminster Abbey, which owned the land. The club was mentioned in a *Cricketers' Guide* of 1851 as being "defective in bowlers", which perhaps led to its demise. However, it was not until the 1880s that most of the houses arrived, and only then that the attractive oval shape was created with gardens in the middle. The street acquired its present name, a distant relation to Primrose Hill, in 1939. Apart from **Nos.56-66**, which are semi-detached stockbroker Tudorish, the houses are in close-knit terraces, some retaining good Victorian detail, for example **No.29**. The 1885-86 Street Directory calls **No.1** a 'collegiate school', and it still bears the inscription "Stanley House School for Boys". The Gardens have recently acquired a wild cherry tree "planted by Mabel Groves", says the plaque, "on her 102nd birthday".

At the far (south) end are the two arms of **ELIZABETH MEWS**, taking their name from Elizabeth Terrace in England's Lane. T G Randall was a prominent butcher in the Terrace, who had his abattoirs in the Mews. But most of the lock-ups here were for cab proprietors, hence the granite setts in the roadway, which were helpful for cab horses. In the 1920s, Victory Garage offered more modern horse-power in its "Daimler Landaulettes – driven by life-experienced chauffeurs". Most of these businesses have now given way to small workshops and bijou residences.

We reach **ENGLAND'S LANE**, one of the older by-ways of this area. It is shown on Rocque's map of 1745 and started life as the pathway that led to Upper Chalcots Farm, situated at the western end of the lane (then rather longer than it is now). The farm's name appeared as Chaldecote in records of 1253 and became Chalcotes in 1531. Robert Morden's map of Middlesex in 1680 is one of the first to show both Upper and Lower Chalcotes, and it was the latter, on the edge of Primrose Hill, that turned into Chalk Farm. In 1776, the upper farm was leased to a James England, hence the road's present name. The 1841 Census includes this name, but some later maps show it mistakenly as Ingram's Lane or Angram's Lane.

In the 1850s, apart from the farm, there were two houses in the Lane –Wychcombe, once used as a School for Young Ladies, and North Hall, for many years the home of the landscape artist Edmund J Niemann (1813-76), whose pictures are, says the DNB unfairly, "at once dexterous and depressing". By 1870 building had begun at the west end of the Lane with the two terraces of shops, called **Elizabeth Terrace**, which have kept their original balconies. **No.40** has been in the butchery business since the late 1860s. Several other businesses have kept their names and natures for over a century, including the pharmacy at **No.28**, which has preserved its decorative shopfront. The **Washington** public house at the west end of the Lane is named after the birthplace in Sussex of the busy developer, Daniel Tidey, who also built the local shops. But an old picture of George Washington (winking), has been preserved on the frontage. The pub is a Listed Building, dated c.1865, and noted as having "vermiculated rustication to the windows".

The south side of the road has made handsome provision for artists over the years, including the Centre Studios of Hampstead Fine Arts College, next to **No.41**. **CHALCOT GARDENS**, set back from the Lane behind trees, was built in the 1880s and named after the farm. **No.16** has the initials of the artist, Adolphus Jacob Whalley: the side extension, dated 1898, was designed by the distinguished C F A Voysey. A better-known artist and illustrator, Arthur Rackham (blue plaque), lived here between 1903 and 1920. **No.15**, built by Batterbury & Huxley, shows its date (1883) over the door, and in its attractive pargetting frieze the initials of another artist, Hal Ludlow. Eight of the other houses were the work of William Willett senior.

A narrow lane (with original lamp bracket at the entrance) leads to **Wychcombe Studios**, which were built by Thomas Batterbury and named after the house on this site. Batterbury's initials (TDB) can be seen on **No.3**, dated 1880. The impressively modern **No.6** arrived in 1989. Norman Wilkinson, the marine artist, was at **No.2** before WWI: his scheme for 'dazzle painting' merchant ships to protect them from submarine attack earned him the OBE. In recent times the sculptor Alan Durst occupied **No.4**. Opposite the studios' entrance, across the road, the building that was the Royal Free Nurses' Home and, long before that, St Mary's Convent School (since 1927 in Fitzjohn's Avenue) is currently a council block of flats for the homeless, grandly named **England's Lane Residence**.

On the left, **ANTRIM ROAD** and at its end **ANTRIM GROVE** started life together in 1897 as Antrim Street, but pressure on the part of the residents caused the change in 1913, and the two sections went their separate ways. Antrim Road is largely occupied by Antrim Mansions, contemporary with the road itself and consisting of several blocks of flats of pleasantly domestic design, enhanced by balconies and evergreens. Here Herbert Farjeon, critic and playwright, lived at **No.45** during WWI and at **No.22**, just before WWII, an even more famous critic, James Agate. But the Mansions' most famous literary figure was Frank Richards (real name Charles Hamilton), creator of Billy Bunter, "Fat Owl of the Remove"; he lived here 1908-11.

At the inner angle of the roads stands the **Belsize Branch Library**, open to the public since April 1897 (**[6]**, p 22) with a short hiatus for rebuilding. The Hampstead Vestry surveyor, aided by the librarian, designed the original building, thus saving the Vestry the cost of an architect. However, in 1925 defects were found in the structure and eleven years later it had to be closed. The present library, opened in March 1937, did have architects – H A Gould and R de W Aldridge, the latter coincidentally being the son of the owner of Antrim Mansions. Pevsner calls it "progressively simple, with apsidal reading room".

The library now has an active supporters' club, Belsize PLUG (Public Library Users' Group), campaigning to preserve this friendly and functional building. Opposite the library is one of the smallest **public gardens** in Hampstead, together with some thriving allotments. This area was used before WWII by Kingsley School of Belsize Park (pp 50-51) as tennis courts. The garden contains a sundial (currently without a dial) made from one of the balusters of old Waterloo Bridge and a stone well-head fashioned from a fragment of the old House of Commons.(A plaque on the well-head verifies this.)

The north-west side of Antrim Grove has some of its original semi-detached villas, **Nos.4-14** with bow windows and hung tiles in small-scale Willett style. On the other side, **No.15** has been described by Cherry and Pevsner as "a small stuccoed house of c.1820, a survivor of the rural villas once scattered over this area". In recent years attempts to demolish the house were rejected by the Council, but rebuilding was allowed as long as the old façade was kept, as "it was too important to the area's architectural heritage to lose".

Turning right, further down Haverstock Hill beyond England's Lane, is Steele's Road, from which stretch at right angles the two branches of **STEELE'S MEWS.** The northern branch retains some of its stables and cobbles, but the southern was rebuilt in 1969-70. **STEELE'S ROAD** originated in 1867 and led to the demolition of the ancient Steele's Cottage (p 17). Several artists' houses, adorned with floral tiles and Queen Anne motifs, were built here in the mid-1870s, again by Batterbury & Huxley. Their north-facing studios are behind. With their variety of detail, stained glass, fanlights and balconies, the houses are now more memorable than the artists who commissioned them. However, they were all respectable and popular artists of their time, frequently on show at the Royal Academy. The elaborate **No.31**, with decorative brick, *de rigueur* sunflower, and date plaque

of 1874, was designed by J M Brydon, architect of Chelsea Town Hall. **No.35 [7]** was built for (Sir) James Linton, first President of the Royal Institute of Painters in Watercolours, and bears a plaque with its date (1875) and his initials. **No.37** was first owned by Frederick Barnard, *Punch* artist and Dickens illustrator, and **No.38** by marine painter Edwin Hayes, whose initials are shown with those of his wife and the date of the house, 1873. **No.39**, which bears its original name, Hawkhurst House, was built for G G Kilburne senior, a watercolorist from Hawkhurst in Kent. Steele's Road has attracted many stars of stage, screen and pop to its handsome houses in recent years.

6 The first foundation stone of Belsize Library being laid in 1896

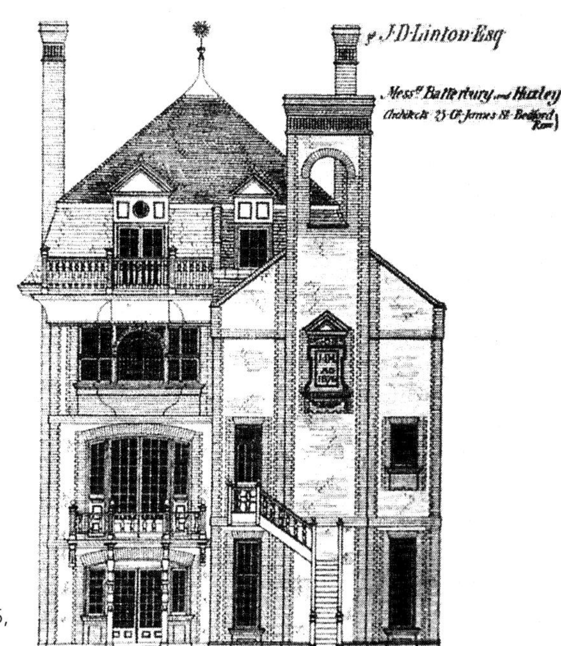

7 No.35 Steele's Road, 1875, by Batterbury & Huxley

Route 3

East of Haverstock Hill

For map see p 10

In this walk, many of the streets cross each other midway along, so a certain amount of map-reading will be necessary.

When in the 1860s William Lund of Haverstock Lodge began to develop his estate on the east side of Haverstock Hill "he publicised the project", says Thompson, "as St John's Park Estate, a title intended to appropriate some of the allure of St John's Wood". The layout was very successful. In particular, Lawn Road, Upper Park Road and Parkhill Road, which followed the existing field lines, created pleasant curves (**[8]**, p 25) and were all laid out on a generous scale. The semi-detached villas were given 50-ft frontages, with ample gaps between the pairs (now haphazardly filled in). The service and mews area for the estate was concentrated in close-packed terrace housing in the Fleet valley, well out of sight. Many of these villas, particularly in Parkhill Road, were built by Richard Batterbury of Camden Town whose son, Thomas Batterbury, was to be responsible for so much artistic building in Hampstead.

Begin at the junction of Haverstock Hill with **DOWNSIDE CRESCENT**, which was built over the grounds of old Haverstock Lodge and followed the line of the drive up to the house. The earliest indication of the road's existence is in 1897, when it was given its present name which, in the absence of subtler meaning, may merely refer to its hillside situation. Most of the houses were built in 1906. The eminent war correspondent Henry Woodd Nevinson, known as 'the Grand Duke', lived at **No.4** for many years, and died there in 1941. He was father to the artist C R W Nevinson (see p 16), and wrote a famous autobiography, *Fire of Life*. In Edwardian times, **No.23** was the home of Thomas Wise, a remarkable collector and seller of antique books, some of which were eventually proved to have been printed by himself. **Nos.15** and **31** have kept most of their original frontages, including doors with stained-glass panels and tile-work pathways.

LAWN ROAD was laid out in the early 1860s across the lawns of Haverstock Lodge, but many of the houses did not follow until the end of the century. In fact, there is an extraordinary diversity of style and period here, from late Victorian semi-detached stucco, through Edwardian Willett-like villas, into 1930s Modernist, and on to a 1960s Council tower block. **Du Maurier House** commemorates the famous family, of whom three generations (George, Gerald and Daphne) had close Hampstead connections. **Cayford House**, Hampstead's first skyscraper, celebrates the local Alderman Florence Cayford. On the east side, **No.27** was the home in recent years of Eva Collet Reckitt of the Reckitt's Blue family: she founded Collet's, the celebrated left-wing bookshop in Charing Cross Road. At the southern end, the Council block **Troyes House** took its name from the previous occupants of the site, the Sisters of Bon Secours de Troyes. Their convent was destroyed by a bomb in 1940, when five nuns were killed. In the same raid was destroyed No.3, briefly the home of Algernon Blackwood, writer of occult novels. On the west side, John Logie Baird, the television pioneer, lived at **No.84** in the 1930s. Many of the neighbouring houses have attractive frontages, endowed with privet hedges and grassy banks. **Nos.79** and **80** are examples of the Edwardian version of 'sweetness and light'.

However, the main architectural interest of Lawn Road is the Grade I-Listed **Isokon** block of flats **[9]** at the north end of the road. Jack Pritchard, who founded the Isokon plywood furniture firm, using designs by Marcel Breuer and the Bauhaus architect Walter Gropius, commissioned Wells Coates in 1934 to build the flats, partly to house refugee artists – such as Gropius and Breuer. Built in concrete, in functional style, Isokon was recognised by Pevsner as "a milestone in the introduction of the modern idiom into London" and "direct to the verge of brutality". The block included the Isobar Club, designed by Breuer and boasting Philip Harben as chef. Among other residents were the artist Adrian Stokes, the constructivist sculptors Laszló Moholy-Nagy and Naum Gabo, and the writers Nicholas Monsarrat and Agatha Christie (it was she who compared the building's exterior to an ocean liner). The flats, which were voted second in *Horizon*'s Ugliest Building Competition of 1946, were bought by *The New Statesman* in 1969 and sold to Camden Council in 1972. After many years of dilapidation and neglect, the flats were taken over and renovated by the Notting Hill Housing Trust. A majority of the 36 flats are earmarked for public service workers.

At the north end of the road **No.50** is at the former entrance to the Fever Hospital, which was on the site of the present Royal Free. A temporary smallpox hospital was built on this site in 1870. It survived until 1872, unlike some of the local inhabitants, who were fatally infected by the disease. This danger was the main objection made to the proposed building of a bigger and better North Western Fever Hospital here in 1874. Protesters said that the site was too near many local schools and the crowds flocking to the Heath. Landowners objected that there would be "ruinous depreciation of valuable property". Such losses would be worse in Belsize, they pointed out, "because the salubrious and select character of the neighbourhood had induced most persons to pay much more for their property than

8 Part of Weller's map of 1862

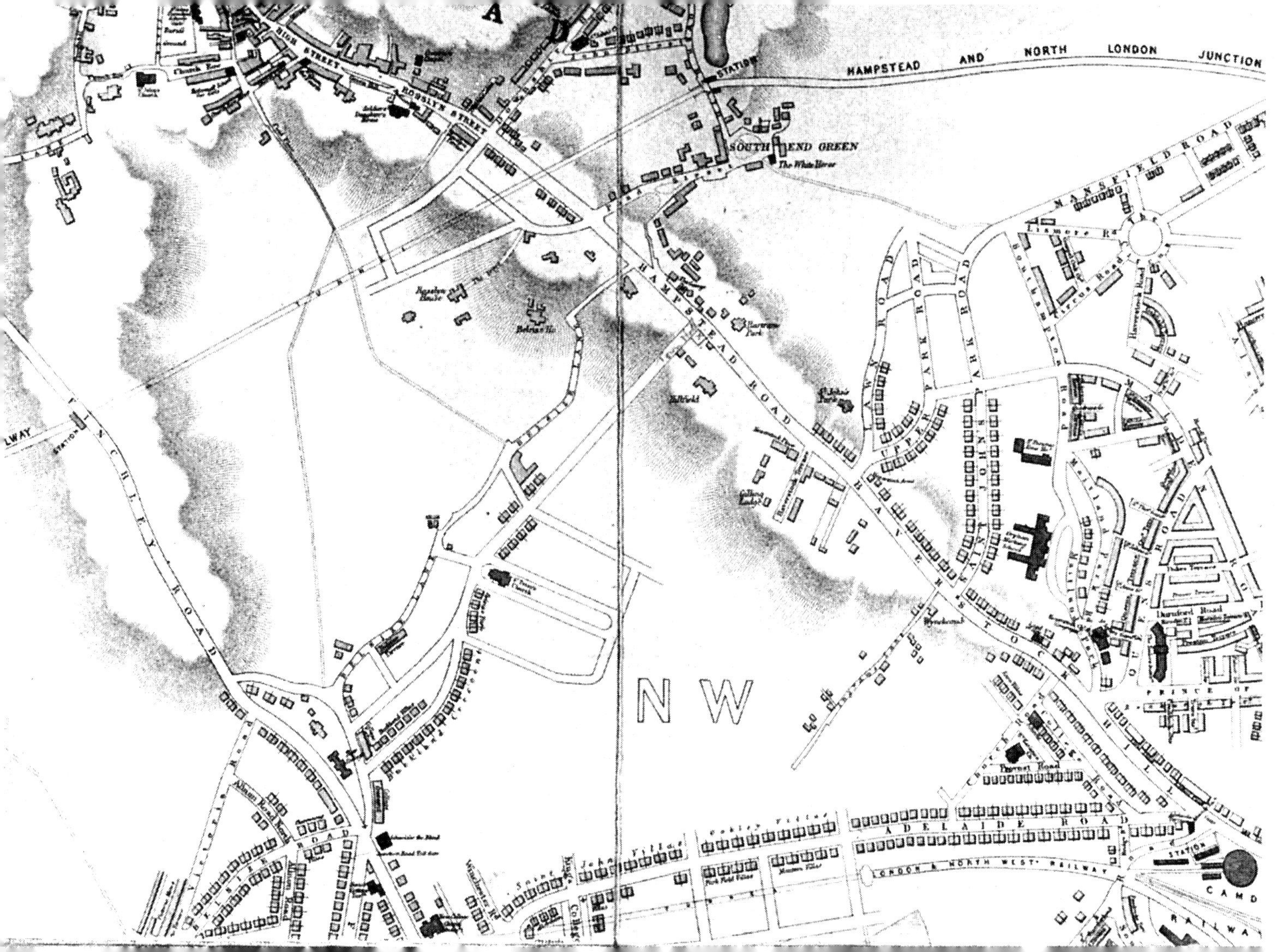

HAMPSTEAD AND NORTH LONDON JUNCTION
HIGH STREET
ROSSLYN STREET
SOUTH END GREEN
The White Horse
MANSFIELD ROAD
HAMPSTEAD ROAD
HAVERSTOCK HILL
UPPER PARK ROAD
PARK ROAD
FINCHLEY ROAD
NW
ADELAIDE ROAD
LONDON & NORTH WEST RAILWAY
STATION
CAMD
RAILWA
Belsize Ho.
Hillfield
Haverstock
Fitzroy Road
Gosier Villas
Saint John's Villas
PRINCE OF

they would have done elsewhere". Delayed by many powerful opponents, including Sir Rowland Hill (p 11), the hospital was not built until 1882, and for some years afterwards the Metropolitan Asylums Board was much criticised for admitting smallpox and fever cases there.

Opposite Isokon, **GARNETT ROAD** was, like Lawn Road, started in the 1860s, and changed its name at frequent intervals. After periods as St Anne's Terrace and Springfield Terrace it was shown as Lower Cross Road on the 1895 Ordnance Survey. Its present name arrived only in 1934 and honours Dr Richard Garnett (1835-1906), who lived for many years in this area and died in Tanza Road (p 82). Garnett spent most of his working life at the British Museum Library, rising to be Keeper of Printed Books in 1890, and in his spare time wrote poetry, biography and critical works. (He was grandfather of the novelist David Garnett.) Among many other local activities, he was president of the Hampstead Antiquarian and Historical Society. "Your tireless feet trod heights we could not reach…" said the farewell ode in the *Hampstead Annual* of 1906-7. Down to earth again the refenestrated and finely refurbished **Park Dwellings** are an early block of Council flats, designed by the Borough Engineer O E Winter, and with a foundation stone laid by

9 The Isokon flats, Lawn Road (Wells Coates, 1934)

the Mayor in 1905. Another block, **Garnett House**, was erected in 1939 on the site of an open-air gymnasium known locally as Jimmie's. **Nos.1-11** arrived in the 1930s and have mostly kept the period flavour of their curved windows.

Turn right into **UPPER PARK ROAD**, which was laid out in 1867 and mainly built up by Richard Batterbury. The road remained totally respectable and middle-class for about 20 years, when the working-class district of Fleet Road began to impinge. An outraged resident wrote to the ground landlord, the Dean and Chapter of Westminster, in 1889, complaining about the erection of "houses of an inferior design, with shops, and a flaring Public House or Gin Palace". Towards the north end of the street now stand the Council flats **Barn Field**, whose prominent ironwork combines the functional with the ornamental. The block was named after a field shown on the manor map of 1762. The artist (Sir) William Coldstream lived in a house here in the 1930s, with the poet W H Auden as lodger and the composer Benjamin Britten on the floor above.

During WWII, **No.36**, formerly a doctor's surgery, housed the Free German League of Culture's Little Theatre. Featuring performances by refugee actors, the theatre could seat 80 spectators and had a 20-square-foot stage. Twelve major productions were mounted between 1940 and March 1946, with Dame Sybil Thorndike as a regular guest artist. The theatre was enlarged in 1943 and abandoned in 1947. Like many other houses in the road, **No.30** has kept its Corinthian columns and wrought-iron pot-guards. From 1933 to 1937, this was the home of Stella Gibbons, author of *Cold Comfort Farm*. She moved here from Fitzjohn's Avenue (p 61) and used this and other Hampstead backgrounds in her writings. The garden of **No.26** was featured in a book published in 1927, *My Town Garden*, by Lady Frances Seton, who wrote vividly about her 'adventures in London clay'.

One of the first inhabitants of **No.8** was Professor Henry Morley (1822-94), the editor of Dickens's periodicals and of *Morley's Universal Library* of English literature. In 1896 his own vast and valuable library was bought by Hampstead Vestry and became the nucleus of the new Central Public Library, opened in Arkwright Road the following year. **No.6** has been restored to its original form and colour and shows what the villas on the estate originally looked like before their yellow brick turned grey.

At the junction with Haverstock Hill, turn left and, shortly after the traffic lights, left again into **PARKHILL ROAD**, which was first called Park Road (hence Upper Park Road, formed later). This was again built up mostly by Richard Batterbury from 1862, being the first development on the St John's Park Estate. Many of the original semi-detached, 4-storey houses have kept up appearances, and the road is enriched by a number of mature trees. **Nos.1A** and **1B**, Danehurst Cottage and Tower Cottage, constitute a mini-chateau dated 1884, which has survived even though Danehurst itself (112 Haverstock Hill), to which it was attached, has gone. The remaining cottages bear the arms of Danehurst's owner, Sir George Barham, founder and chairman of Express Dairies and Mayor of Hampstead in 1905. His crest shows three bears (probably a rebus for Bear-Home = Barham), two martlets, a stork (see also the stabling in Akenside Road, p 61) and some bulrushes. Thomas Danby, the artist son of the more famous Francis, died at **No.11** in 1886. Apart from his landscapes in the style of Claude, he was well known as a skittle player at the Bull & Bush at North End.

The sculptor Henry Moore and his wife Irina lived at **No.11A** from 1929 to 1940, as the recently erected blue plaque records. When this house was bombed in 1940, he moved briefly to the Mall Studios (p 29) and then to Hertfordshire. It was at No.11A that Moore first experimented with driving holes through his sculptures and developed his distinctive abstract style. **No.13** was the home of senior postal official F E Baines in 1889, when he completed his monumental *Records of Hampstead*, published the following year. The well-designed **Rose Bush Court**, flats for the elderly, is not just a pretty name but commemorates Miss Rose Bush of the

10 Parkhill Road Studios, c.1880, on the site of Wood Field

Humanist Society, which built the block. Behind here is the unexpectedly large **Three Acres Play Project**, a popular Council-run youth scheme, using grounds vacated by the Belsize Tennis Club. Next door, **Allison Court** has embraced the original **No.43**, offering residents a choice between 19th- and 20th-century styles. Higher up, **Wood Field**, a post-WWII Council block, fits unobtrusively into the road pattern, helped by its old trees. At the northern end of Parkhill Road, the 1885 Directory shows Parkhill Road Studios **[10]** and the stables of the London Street Tramways Co.

On the eastern side of the road, a new block of flats, **No.84**, has been built on the site of the century-old Parkhill Garden Nursery. Beside an entry to Dunboyne Road (see *Streets of Gospel Oak and West Kentish Town*), an iron Hampstead parish **boundary post**, marked HP 1824, was possibly wrongly placed here in 1890 when the Hampstead/St Pancras borders were re-drawn. (Parts of Southampton Road, together with Kingsford Street and the new Dunboyne Road belong to Hampstead but are post-coded NW5.) In a neighbourhood noted for its starving artists, **No.80** was in 1900 a Home for Lost and Starving Cats. The Dutch painter Piet Mondrian lived at **No.60** (see plaque) from 1938 until it was bombed in 1940. His studio overlooked Barbara Hepworth's in the Mall Studios, and she has described how he took over a dreary room, painted it white, and "his wonderful squares of primary colours climbed up the walls". The showy squashed-looking **No.30A** is called Nightingale House, after its owner and co-architect. Cherry/Pevsner found it "cleverly planned". Charles Williams (1885-1945), the versatile author and vigorous theologian, had a top-floor flat at **No.18** from 1917 to 1939. W H Auden met Williams locally in the 1930s and was struck by his "highly idiosyncratic and romantic view" of the Christian religion. "For the first time in my life", he wrote, "I felt myself in the presence of personal sanctity".

TASKER ROAD crosses Parkhill Road roughly in the middle and leads to the back of St Dominic's Priory. It is shown as Church Road on the 1866 map and got its present name only in 1937. It now commemorates Countess Tasker, who contributed largely to the building of the Priory. **Parkhill Walk** is a gated enclave of modern houses, apparently built into the back gardens of Parkhill Road.

On the other side of Tasker Road are the famous **Mall Studios**, a stable-like terrace of seven cottages with an eighth standing sentinel at the end of the path. They were built by Thomas Batterbury in 1872, and he remained the owner until his death in 1922. (A detailed history of the Studios appears in *Camden History Review* No.8, 1980.) Early occupants included Sir George Clausen (see p 14), Robert Macbeth, described by the *DNB* as 'an able etcher', Thomas Danby and, in the early 1900s, Arthur Rackham. The abstract painter Cecil Stephenson took over **No.8** from Walter Sickert in 1919 and stayed until his death in 1965.

The most significant period for the Mall, however, was in the 1930s. From 1927 to 1932, Studio **No.2** was occupied by the sculptors John Skeaping and his wife Barbara Hepworth, and then by her and her second husband, Ben Nicholson: their triplets were born here in 1934. After they all left for Cornwall in 1940, Henry Moore briefly used the studio. The occupant of **No.3** in the 1930s was (Sir) Herbert Read, the poet and critic. In an article on *Art in Britain 1930-40*, he wrote about artists in the Mall, Isokon and neighbouring areas "living and working together in Hampstead, as closely and intimately as artists of Florence and Siena had lived and worked in the Quattrocentro...Within this inner group that worked within five minutes' walking distance of each other in Hampstead I do not remember any quarrels, any jealousy or spitefulness. It was a 'nest' of gentle artists...The war came and destroyed it all. Such a feeling of unanimity was never to come again after the war, but English art had come of age."

Route 4

The Eton College Estate, South

From Chalk Farm Underground to the Swiss Cottage Centre

This walk begins at Chalk Farm Underground station, where Adelaide Road debouches into Haverstock Hill. Until the 1820s the southern part of Hampstead was almost entirely rural (see Weller's map, **[8]**, p 25). Apart from the Belsize estate, the most notable landmark in the area was the Chalcots estate (later known as Chalk Farm), 243 acres of land owned since 1449

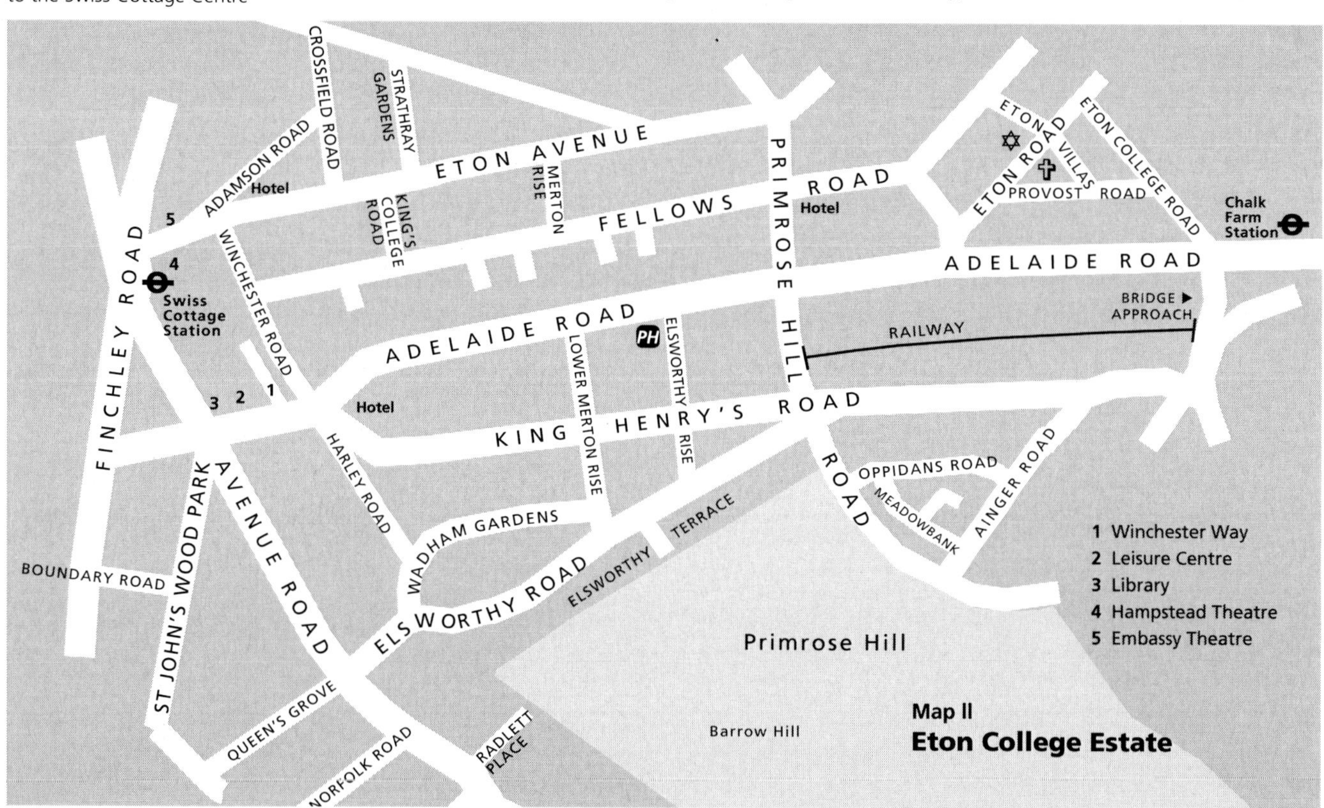

Map II
Eton College Estate

by Eton College. In 1820, when Nash's Regent's Park redevelopment was nearing completion, builders and landowners began to look to the area north of the park for further terrain. The Eton land was surveyed in 1824 and found "suitable for villa development". An Act of Parliament was passed authorising the College to grant building leases, and in 1829 a 15-acre site adjoining Haverstock Hill was offered to builders in half-acre plots.

Further development was complicated by the coming of the railways and by a scheme to turn Primrose Hill into a cemetery (see p 35). It was another 10 years before building began. Many of these buildings were destroyed in WWII, and in 1965 the whole central area of 35 acres was re-planned by Camden Council as the new Chalcots Estate. The additional demolition of existing houses and shops, especially those of King's College Road (p 40), caused considerable protest. In 1992, management of the Chalcot Park Estate was passed to the Hampstead Garden Suburb Trust (the Suburb itself was built on land owned by the College), but in the next few years the college sold off the bulk of its property. By 1995 over 1000 residential properties had been sold, and after five and a half centuries the Eton connection was ended.

ADELAIDE ROAD has had a difficult history. It was one of the earliest roads to be constructed in the area, actually started by Eton College in 1830, and named after William IV's newly crowned Queen. But no houses were built until nine years later, when Samuel Cuming began to line the road with his Late Classical residences.

The Queen was also commemorated in the Adelaide Tavern **[11]** which, being a public house, was one of the first buildings in the street. The already derelict tavern was destroyed by fire in 1985, but the

11 The Adelaide tavern, burnt down 1985

new **No.1** has reproduced some of the old building's frontage; here are now flats and shops and fast-food parlours. "The Adelaide" is now the name of another pub much higher up the road; it originated in the 1850s as The Viceroy.

Adelaide Road was still not complete when the London and Birmingham Railway, which runs parallel to it, was opened in 1837. The **Primrose Hill Tunnel**, 1164 yards long between Primrose Hill Road and Alexandra Road NW8, was considered a triumph of engineering; it was London's first railway tunnel, and crowds gathered along Adelaide Road to watch its construction. Robert Stephenson's secretary, W H Budden, designed the magnificent turreted stone front (**[12]**, p 34) to the tunnel, which has since been doubled in width to allow for more traffic. Its rugged design was said to be intended to give confidence to the new breed of railway passenger. (The tunnels were Listed in 1974.)

Chalk Farm Station on the Northern Line of the Underground was opened in 1907 and has kept much of its original design, including ox-blood tiles, ox-eye windows and heavy eyebrows. Sadly, when the station was rebuilt in 1986, it lost some attractive details such as the *art nouveau* ticket office.

Turning right from the station entrance we glance at the terrace of houses across Adelaide Road, **Nos.23-49**, which show what the early buildings in this quiet, middle-class road looked like. They were quickly taken by lawyers, surgeons, teachers of music, dancing or languages, and proprietors of private schools, which usually had only a brief life. The road's famous inhabitants did not stay here long either. The artist and inventor William de Morgan spent some of his youth here, but Mary Webb, Cecil Sharp, William Dobson and Stanley Spencer soon found better accommodation in other parts of Hampstead. All their residences have now disappeared, as has No.69, which was the home of the 'figurative abstract' artist Ivon Hitchens, from 1919 until he was bombed out in 1940. His musical mural is a famous feature of Cecil Sharp House in Regent's Park Road. Many other houses near the junction with Primrose Hill Road were also bombed.

On the right-hand side the even-numbered houses have been replaced by handsome 1950s blocks of flats, the first one designed by Louis de Soissons and named **Constable House** in honour of the Borough's most eminent artist. After this comes an attractive late-1970s low-rise development named **Beaumont Walk,** containing pathways inscribed with poetic gems ranging from Wordsworth to Spike Milligan. Across the road you will see the trees of the **Adelaide Nature Reserve**, open on Tuesdays all day and for special events at other times; this protects a modicum of wild life, including dragonflies and newts, on a narrow strip of hilly woodland between road and railway. Further up the road on that (southern) side you can see the first of the 20-storey Council tower blocks, **Blashford.** On the northern side of Adelaide Road rear up another four: **Dorney**, **Bray**, **Burnham** and **Taplow** (named from east to west), designed by Dennis Lennon as part of the Chalcots Estate redevelopment beginning in 1965. They were all named after villages near Eton (Bray is famous for its Vicar and Burnham for its beeches).

Turn back alongside the Nature Reserve. The space between it and No.49 is earmarked for a new synagogue, transferred from Eton Road (p 43). After No.23 turn right up **BRIDGE APPROACH,** which is shown in the 1854 Directory as Bridge Road, Adelaide Road, and did not get its present name until 1936. The bridge at the top of the road was built over the London & Birmingham Railway in 1839 by Robert Stephenson. It was his first iron bridge, and the prototype of larger ones to follow at Newcastle and the Menai Straits. Primrose Hill Station below it opened here in 1851, but "trains don't stop here anymore" and the station entrance has been turned to commercial use. On the right is the gate of **Iron Bridge House,** built by the LMS Railway in the early 1920s as a staff hostel for long-distance train drivers. It was converted into offices by Victor

Wybrow in the late 1980s. Next door, **No.1** was in the 1850s the home of Samuel Cuming, the ubiquitous local developer.

Cross the bridge (which can now be crossed only on foot, bike or fire engine), admiring the imaginative murals painted in 2007 by the Primrose Hill Association Volunteers, led by Maureen Betts, and turn right into **KING HENRY'S ROAD**; this was originally a road of semi-detached villas which has been semi-destroyed by developers, Councils and the bombs of WWII. At this corner is one of the earliest buildings in the street – the Boys' Home of 1865 (see *Primrose Hill to Euston Road)*, which was converted into flats called **The Chesterfields** in 1982. King Henry's Road (the eponymous king is Henry VI, founder of Eton College) was begun by Samuel Cuming in 1856 and, according to Thompson, continued into the 1870s by Robert Yeo in "a good deal more skimped and debased" style. **No.17** was the home of Elizabeth Lutyens, daughter of the architect Sir Edwin. She composed hundreds of works, ranging from string quartets to scores for horror films: she died here in 1983. The blue plaque on **No.10** salutes Dr Bhimrao Ambedkar (1891-1956), Indian crusader for social justice, who lived here 1921-22. **Nos.29-49** and some of the houses opposite have kept their original façades, with many a Corinthian capital. Oskar Kokoschka, the Austrian expressionist painter, lived briefly at **No.45A** at the beginning of WWII. In the early 1960s, Glenda Jackson, then a struggling actress (later film star and then MP for Hampstead and Highgate), occupied a bed-sitter near here. Further west, **Primrose Hill Court**, designed by Douglas & Wood, was erected by Hampstead Borough Council in 1951 (see plaque in archway) on an area that was devastated by a flying bomb in 1944.

A side-road to the left leads to one entrance to Primrose Hill Workshops, **No.77** (the other being in Oppidans Road), and an enclave of small houses with tiny gardens, **Nos.79-87**. The Council flats at No.89, called **Whitton** mark the site of Myra Lodge, the residence of Miss Frances Buss, founder of the North London Collegiate and the Camden School for Girls. A great pioneer of education for women, she used Myra Lodge and two adjoining houses for boarders at her Camden Town school from 1868 until her death in 1894.

We have reached Primrose Hill Road. Turn left up the hill and after a short distance left again into **OPPIDANS ROAD**. Named after the town-boarders of Eton College and laid out in the late 1860s, this road immediately attracted respectable residents. Among stories about the above-mentioned Miss Buss is one of her encounter with a little girl from Oppidans Road, who had lost her nanny in a game of hide-and-seek in the Chalk Farm railway coalyards. Asked where she lived, the tearful girl could only say, "Near some red mountains", which Miss Buss rightly interpreted as the new houses being built near Primrose Hill. The south side of the road has kept most of its original stock-brick houses. The north side was much affected by the flying bomb in 1944, and now includes the Nissen-type **Primrose Hill Workshops**. Oppidans Mews has disappeared under a branch of **MEADOWBANK**, a street of houses and flats filled in between Oppidans and Ainger Roads. It has swept away the houses of Primrose Hill Road's most famous residents. Fred Terry, the actor-manager, and Julia Neilson, his partner both on and off the stage, lived at No.4 for many years. Adelina Patti (1843-1919), the coloratura soprano, was briefly at No.8, before retreating to her castle in South Wales, and Helen Waddell, scholar and writer, bought No.32 very soon after publication of her successful novel *Peter Abelard* (1933). She stayed in this "large, damp house that proved an unending source of trouble and expense" until shortly before her death in 1965.

We turn right out of Oppidans Road into **AINGER ROAD**. This was first called Windsor Road, but was finally named after a master at Eton, A C Ainger, who wrote the school song. As Ainger was also the name of a popular vicar of Hampstead Parish Church, it is possible that the authorities were killing two birds with one street-name. The road appeared first in the 1869 Directory and included the inevitable **AINGER MEWS** and a temporary iron church, the precursor of St Mary's, Primrose Hill (p 35). The priest-in-charge lived at **No.9 AINGER ROAD**, surrounded (in 1885) mainly by small tradesmen (builder, greengrocer, tailor, dressmaker), but also by a bandmaster and a mineral-water manufacturer.

12 Portal of Primrose Hill Tunnel, 1837

The solid stock-brick houses have mostly kept some pleasant period features, such as their windows and pot-holders.

Ainger Road opens onto the side of Primrose Hill, so named in the reign of Elizabeth I. "Methinks it is a pleasant thing to walk on Primrose Hill", says a ballad of around 1620, and there were plenty of primroses to pick at the time. Now the hill has been deflowered and its junior partner, known as Barrow Hill (meaning a wooded hill, not a burial mound), has been flattened to hold a reservoir. This is presumed to be 'The Barrow', mentioned in a 10th-century document describing the boundaries of Hampstead. For some time, a stone in the ditch by the north fence of the reservoir marked the spot where Sir Edmund Berry Godfrey was found one morning in 1678, with his neck broken and a sword through his body. One theory was that he was implicated in a Catholic plot to overthrow Charles II, but the truth was never established, although three men were hanged for the crime. In the 18th and early 19th centuries, the area round Primrose Hill and Chalk Farm became notorious as duelling grounds. In a more peaceful vein, William Blake had a vision on the hill of "the spiritual sun – not like a golden disc the size of a guinea but like an innumerable company of the heavenly host crying 'Holy, holy, holy'."

In the 1830s, when cemeteries were being laid out all round London, including the one in Highgate, commercial eyes were cast on Primrose Hill. It was fashionable to have a tomb with a view, and the Portland Cemetery Bill was introduced in Parliament in 1837. The Bill, which would have allowed the enclosure of Primrose Hill, passed a second reading and committee. However, local people then became aware of the threat to an important beauty spot and caused the Vestry to oppose the Bill. The matter became one of national importance and, in the public agitation that followed, the Government was persuaded to secure Primrose Hill for public use. In 1842, Eton gave up 53 acres of Primrose Hill in exchange for 32 acres of Crown land near the College.

Barratt records the elaborate ceremony of planting an oak on the hill for the 1864 Shakespeare tercentenary. This was attended by an impressive procession of the Working Men's Shakespeare Celebration Committee, who had marched from Russell Square and apparently gave some people the erroneous impression that they were leading a protest on behalf of Garibaldi. Another oak was planted in 1964 in a simpler ceremony. In recent years, the hill has become the venue for Druids' rites at midsummer, while other exercises are performed in the open-air **gymnasium** erected in 1847, adjoining the playground.

At the junction with **PRIMROSE HILL ROAD** we turn right and return down the hill. On the left, at the corner with Elsworthy Road, stands the 1872 French Gothic basilica of **St Mary the Virgin**, designed by architect Michael Manning, who lived in Provost Road (p 44). Many attractive features of the interior were designed by other local artists – the reredos and pulpit by G F Bodley, oak seating by Temple Moore, stained glass by Clayton & Bell, and enamel work by Henry Holiday (see the church's admirable guidebook). From 1865, services had been held in premises in King Henry's Road and Ainger Road. The Rev. C J Fuller moved with his flock to St Mary's when it opened, but he incurred the displeasure of his bishop because of his High Church practices, and it was not until 1885, when Dr Frederick Temple became Bishop of London, that the church was consecrated. From 1901 to 1915 the vicar, Percy Dearmer, chief editor of the *English Hymnal* and *Songs of Praise*, "made the church a showpiece of liturgical worship and good music." His reforms included the whitewashing of the interior, which was originally dark red and black. Dearmer commissioned Ralph Vaughan Williams as composer for the new English Hymnal. Plaques commemorate Dearmer and his organist, another local recruit, Martin Shaw, 'Master of the Music, 1909-20'. In 1956, St Paul's parish joined St Mary's, having lost its church in Avenue Road (p 38); a model of that church is part of the statue of St Paul at the west end of St Mary's. In 2007 the old choir vestry was rebuilt for community use as St Mary's Centre. The recently restored WWI memorial at the corner of Elsworthy Road includes Dearmer's wife Mabel and their son Christopher.

Beyond the church, a little further along Primrose Hill Road are to be seen (on the left) the first white blocks in a series of attractive weatherboarded estates that stretch along the north side of King Henry's Road all the way to its junction with Adelaide Road at its western end. They are low-rise because of being built over the Primrose Hill Tunnel; this is also the reason why the four tower blocks mentioned on p 32 were built to the north of Adelaide Road. The eastern portal of the tunnel (**[12]**, p 34) lies under the right-hand side of the roadway here, but it cannot be seen from where we stand. Street names within the estate continue the Eton associations – **QUICKSWOOD**, **CONYBEARE**, **HAWTREY ROAD** and **ELLIOTT SQUARE** bear names of former provosts or vice-provosts of the College. **LYTTELTON CLOSE** at the far end recalls Edward Lyttelton, son of the fourth Baron and headmaster of Eton 1905-16. Quickswood is on the site of old No.98, where Marie Lloyd, the music-hall legend, lived in great style (real Chippendale in the dining room) in Edwardian times.

We, however, turn into **ELSWORTHY ROAD** on the south side of the church. This and a little side-shoot, Elsworthy Terrace, were built by 1885, and the road then ended at Lower Merton Rise (p 37). Beyond this, Elsworthy Road was laid out across the old Eton & Middlesex Cricket Ground from 1890, but was not complete until 1915 (see later). The derivation of the street name is not clear, and Eton College Library has not been able to shed any light on it. First on the corner is **Elsworthy Court**, in which No.1 was for many years the home of Professor William Grimes, the distinguished archaeologist, who excavated the bomb-shattered City after WWII, and discovered, among other relics, the Temple of Mithras.

Most of the original houses in Elsworthy Road are still standing, but Nos.1-5 have been replaced by **St Paul's C of E Primary School**, which moved here from Winchester Road (p 40) in 1972. The school began in a house in King's College Road Mews (p 40) in 1870. Sir Henry Wood, the conductor (1869-1944), lived at **No.4** from 1905 to 1937 (see plaque). He was musical director of the Promenade Concerts at the Queen's Hall from 1895, and under him they became an annual institution. His house was much visited by Richard Strauss and other composers, and he once lent it to Delius. This and adjoining houses have curious goblin-like corbels at first floor level, and nearly all the other houses in the street are of some aesthetic or curiosity value to the passing pedestrian. **Nos.7-15** offer a wide variety of quirky doorways and other decorations.

Opposite the modern block Nos.17-19, **ELSWORTHY RISE** runs northwards to King Henry's Road and through to Adelaide Road. This, like Lower Merton Rise further west (p 31), was designed for tradesmen, shopkeepers and stable owners to service the local middle-class residents. Elsworthy Rise was formerly Eton Place and appeared as such in the 1873 Directory. At that date, the builder Samuel Cuming is shown as a resident, together with a stables, a decorator and a plumber. By 1885, the amusingly named King Henry's Nursery is shown on the west side.

Back in Elsworthy Road, we come shortly to **ELSWORTHY TERRACE**, whose **No.1** shows dragonhead water-spouts. The Terrace leads invitingly to Primrose Hill, with rather grander houses on the east side than the west. A recent resident of the Terrace was the film director Sam Mendes while, round the corner, paparazzi were besieging the home of rock star Liam Gallagher and actress Patsy Kensit. On the north side of the road, **Nos.26-32** show the variegated pleasures of early Willett architecture: floral and faunal embellishment, tile-hung facades, semi-Moorish arches and mythical beasts.

Most of the houses to the west of Elsworthy Terrace were erected by William Willett, Junior, with Amos Faulkner as architect, "putting Norman Shaw on the production line", as Thompson styled it. Shaw was the champion of the Queen Anne Revival, already popular in northern Hampstead, and now adapted by Faulkner in the south with a great variety of roofline and red brick exteriors. Pevsner says Faulkner was employing "the comfortably relaxed eclecticism of the Arts and Crafts movement in almost indigestible profusion". For his sensitive and generous layout of 'Elsworthy Village', with its wide pavements, plane trees and privet hedges, Wm Willett Jr was hailed as "the pioneer of garden suburb development". Sir Raymond Unwin acknowledged his debt to him when designing Hampstead Garden Suburb. At the time of the Elsworthy project, Willett senior (1837-1913) was handing over to his eponymous son (1856-1915), who was a fanatical early riser, and an untiring advocate of Daylight Saving and Summer Time. He died just before Parliament made his scheme legal in 1916. **No.25 ELSWORTHY ROAD** was built by Batterbury & Huxley (pp 9, 73), an odd incursion into Willett-land, as was **No.33** by Stevenson & Redfern.

On the northern side, No.40 is on the corner with **LOWER MERTON RISE**. Merton Road, named after Eton College's Merton Priory Estate at Windsor, originally ran between Adelaide Road and King Henry's Road only. It was extended south to Elsworthy Road by 1894 and north to Eton Avenue by 1915, and it was renamed Merton Rise in 1937. But this southern segment had to be rechristened in 1972 after being divorced from its upper half by the Chalcots Estate development (p 31). William de Morgan, the brilliant ceramicist (1839-1917), came with his family to No.6 Merton Road in the 1860s but, after his father died in 1871, moved on to Chelsea. **No.1** was adapted in 1944 from the coach house and stables of No.19 Wadham Gardens.

We round the corner and almost immediately turn left into **WADHAM GARDENS**. This was the last road in the area to be developed by Willett Jr at the turn of the 20th century. It may be named after Wadham College, Oxford, but the connection is not clear. The attractive houses were all designed by Amos Faulkner except **No.2**, which was by the local architect Horace Field. The curving road, with its communal garden, plane trees and privet, again demonstrates the pleasures of the garden suburb ideal. **No.30** on the left was the final home of Hans Feibusch, prolific muralist and sculptor: he died here in 1998, aged 99. The elegant **No.19**, opposite, apparently a period Arts and Crafts mansion, was in fact built in 1991 (architects Carden & Godfrey). **No.17** bears its date and the initials of its first owner, Charles Frederick Hardy, and **No.7** has fine plasterwork foliage. **No.4** was for many years the home of Montague Arrobus, the ostrich feather merchant, and of his son Sydney, a popular local artist.

Swinging round to the left over a short stretch of Harley Road, we come again to **ELSWORTHY ROAD** and gaze across at handsome **Nos.45-53**, nearly hidden behind what used to be Elsworthy's 'village green', but is now mostly an evergreen copse. The vigorous conductor Sir Georg Solti (1912-97) lived for many years at No.51. Further east, **No.39** is where Sigmund Freud first found shelter when he came as a refugee to Britain in 1938; soon thereafter he moved to Maresfield Gardens (p 59). Behind us, **No.48** has a history: in the early 1930s, it belonged to Viscount Furness, whose wife Thelma had, says the DNB, 'a passing affair' with the Prince of Wales: he was reputedly a frequent visitor to this house (and to at least two other houses in the neighbourhood). When Lady Furness introduced him to her friend and fellow-American, Mrs Wallis Simpson, the future Edward VIII found "the supreme passion of his life".

Return to **HARLEY ROAD** and pass by the end of Wadham Gardens. The road's name again seems to have been taken from Oxford rather than Eton. The Harley family, Earls of Oxford, not only owned the Harley Street area of Marylebone, but had a small estate at the bottom of Avenue Road. The Vestry Minutes of 1862 give the first reference to Harley Road, and the whole street appears in the 1869 Directory. **No.7** was called Compton Lodge in 1901, when Dame Clara Butt came to live here (see plaque), and still bears that name. A memorable contralto, Dame Clara moved in after her marriage to Robert Kennerley Rumford, a forgotten baritone, and stayed until 1929. She was much admired by Elgar, who composed *Sea Pictures* for her, and with whose *Land of Hope and Glory* she thrilled the nation. The house is now a home for the elderly run by Central and Cecil Housing. **Nos.26&28** are both Willett houses belonging to the red-brick south, rather than to the stock-brick north. Much of the west side of the road was demolished during and after WWII. One of the first to live and to die (1885) at the vanished No.4 was Alfred Meeson, architect of the original Alexandra Palace and supervisor under Sir Charles Barry of the building of the present Houses of Parliament: both sites had been the scenes of enormous conflagrations.

At the north-west end of the road, **The Frank Barnes School** is a nursery and primary school for the deaf, purpose-built by the ILEA in 1978, and designed (with special acoustic considerations) by Ivor Plummer. Frank Barnes was head of the first residential school for the deaf set up by the London School Board in 1900, beginning in Homerton, transferring to Islington, and finally moving to Hampstead. Another move is currently on the cards.

Ahead lies the **Marriott Hotel Regents Park** (formerly the Holiday Inn), by Dennis Lennon & Partners 1973 (Pevsner notes its "diffidently frivolous Mediterranean manner, with round-headed arches and a light grid of balconies"). To the left, the tail end of Adelaide Road meets **AVENUE ROAD** at the main traffic junction. This road appears in draft form on Greenwood's map of 1824, but was not developed until after the Finchley Road Act of 1826. Colonel Eyre, who was mainly to benefit from the building of the new road to Finchley, was then able to open up his St John's Wood estate and link it to Regent's Park with a grand avenue. Though the road still maintains a fairly impressive façade, most of its original buildings have gone.

On the south-western border of the area under survey (see map on p 30), the borough boundary first of Hampstead, now of Camden, runs along St Edmund's Terrace, up the middle of Avenue Road, and then zig-zags via Queen's Grove to Finchley Road. It passes through a fragment of **BOUNDARY ROAD**, which marks the border with old St Marylebone (now Westminster), and **ST JOHN'S WOOD PARK**, which commemorates the Knights of St John but is now a forest of flats. There is no trace now of the home of Mrs Henry Wood, author of the heart-rending *East Lynne*, who died here in 1887.

William Collins, the popular landscape artist, lived at the old No.20 Avenue Road in 1839-40, and his son, Wilkie Collins, referred to the road in *The Woman in White*, published in 1862. Walter Hartright, the narrator, who encounters the 'woman in white' in Finchley Road, describes how he accompanied her through the gate of the turnpike at the Swiss Cottage end of Avenue Road. This must have been the northern limit of building, for the woman is agitated by the sight of the gas lamps and says: "This is London." Halfway down Avenue Road on the east side in **Radlett Place** (now NW8) are embedded two **boundary stones**, marked "HP 1838/SMB1842", meaning Hampstead Parish and St Marylebone.

North of this, Sir Alexander Korda, the film producer, lived at the new **No.81 AVENUE ROAD** in the 1930s. Other 20th-century residents of this area have included actors Matheson Lang, Marie Tempest and Sir Cedric Hardwicke, and the gifted chemical industrialists Ludwig and (Sir) Robert Mond. Ludwig bequeathed his fabulous collection of early Italian pictures to the National Gallery. **No.85** stands out for architectural quality – a touch of the Lutyens?

Further north again, on the site of the present **Polygon** flats, was St Paul's Church, built in 1859 by S S Teulon, 10 years before St Stephen's (p 11), but destroyed by bombing in 1940. Pevsner said it had "all Teulon's sense of sensational display".

Near the corner with Adelaide Road,

the **Swiss Cottage School** was opened in 1995 for children with special needs: its success was recognised in 2000 when it became a beacon school. This institution replaced two LCC special schools, the F D Roosevelt opened in 1957 for the physically handicapped, and the John Keats opened in 1959 for delicate children.

North of Adelaide Road, past the public library, in what was originally called Upper Avenue Road, is the **Swiss Cottage Centre**. This area has an impressive record of public service. On the site of the library was a Congregational Chapel (1851). To the north was a hospital, St Columba's, which moved to Spaniards Road in 1956. At the corner with College Crescent, from the 1860s until WWII, was the school of the London Society for Teaching & Training the Blind.

All this 7-acre site was cleared by Hampstead Borough Council in the 1950s to be developed into a civic centre, including a Town Hall and offices. With Basil Spence as its architect, the Council built the **Central Library** (with vertical décor to suggest the leaves of a book) and a Sports Centre, and these were opened by the Queen in 1964. Further plans were complicated by the coming of Camden in 1965, and the original project was abandoned. Part of the site was sold off for an office block in the north-west corner (**No.100** Avenue Road), designed by Ted Levy, Benjamin and Partners. From the late 1990s the Council announced plans to regenerate the Swiss Cottage Centre and by 2007 at a cost of some £85m had achieved a remarkable new look. The Sports Centre was demolished and replaced by a gleaming glass **Leisure Centre**, designed by Sir Terry Farrell. This has two swimming pools and a myriad of other sports facilities, including a climbing wall on the Adelaide Road frontage. The £27m Centre also has 42 affordable flats, a community centre (see p 40) and a doctor's surgery in **Winchester Way**. The social housing was provided by the developers Barratts, who were thereby allowed to build the Visage block of 131 luxury apartments.

Swiss Cottage Park is now the rather optimistic name of the grassy central area, designed by Gusefson Porter, with long rows of tough-looking plants. There is a sporadic water feature/paddling pool, a football/tennis pitch and a play area for small children. The Library also had a make-over in 2002-03, with more light and accessibility, a colourful Children's Library and the Swiss Cottage Art Gallery. Opposite the Library entrance is a bronze abstract sculpture by Frederick McWilliam (1964) called the *Hampstead Figure*, offering a rather bleak welcome to the lively Swiss Cottage Centre.

Route 5

The Eton College Estate, North

For map see p 30

The roads immediately north of Adelaide Road were developed from the 1860s as a residential area, with substantial houses on tree-lined streets like Eton Road and particularly imposing detached houses on broad Eton Avenue. We, however, start with the least leafy road, which was laid out between Adelaide Road and Eton Avenue, namely Fellows Road. This can be reached from a bus stop either on Adelaide Road or on the northern stretch of Primrose Hill Road.

At the corner of Adelaide Road and **PRIMROSE HILL ROAD** is **Rackstraw House**, flats for the elderly built by the Hampstead Old People's Housing Trust, which was founded by Hampstead heroine Marjorie Rackstraw. It is now run by the Central and Cecil Housing Trust. Up the street, the first turn to the left is **FELLOWS ROAD**. This is shown on a map of 1860, but building was not completed until the early 1880s. The large, grey-brick houses, decorated with solid Corinthian capitals, once housed an impressive assemblage of military men, surgeons and lawyers. The street name was chosen for its Etonian connections, the school's governors being called Fellows.

On the north side of the road remain

many of the mid-Victorian houses built by Eton's busy developer Samuel Cuming. The basic austerity of many of these is relieved by decorative touches, such as the Tiffany-type fanlights on **Nos.36-46**. By contrast, the south side of the road has been nearly all redeveloped since WWII as part of the Council's Chalcots Estate redevelopment (p 31). Gone are the homes of Sir Arnold Bax, Master of the Queen's Musick (No.155); of the artist Duncan Grant, beloved by the Bloomsbury set (No.143); the wood-engraving Dalziel Brothers; and artist Francis Barraud (No.107), originator of the HMV (His Master's Voice) trademark. Instead we have a number of modern enclaves or Closes, named **Briary**, **Brocas**, **Huson**, **Hornby** and **Tobin**, the latter commemorating the long-serving local councillor Julian Tobin. The monotony of the north side is broken by two short roads leading to Eton Avenue. The rise and fall of Merton Rise has been described already (p 37). After this come post-bombing blocks of flats, this time in red brick, where once stood the homes of Walter Bayes, a founder member of the Camden Town Group (No.82), and of author Florence Upton, inventor of the Golliwogg (*sic*) (No.76), and a little further on, curiously different **No.100A**, recently labelled Chapel House, in the 1930s the studio of Margaret Fountaine, travel writer, and author of delightful *Love Among the Butterflies*.

The changing fortunes of the second short road, **KING'S COLLEGE ROAD**, were similar to those of Merton Rise. The road and its mews, begun about 1870, housed many builders and gasfitters and eventually garages, notably the anachronistically named King Henry's Garage. All the southern sector, including the mews, was demolished in 1968, and in the northern stretch only two domesticated stables remain. The name of the road has Eton connections again, referring to the first name of the school, King's College of Our Lady of Eton.

The western end of Fellows Road runs into **WINCHESTER ROAD**, which was built by 1862 and named after the first Provost of Eton, William Waynflete, Bishop of Winchester. **Nos.24-32** on the east side show what the original Winchester Road looked like. At the corner is **Mora Burnet House**, sheltered housing built by the Humanist Housing Association in the 1970s and rebuilt recently. To the south of it is the **Winchester Project**, based in a late Victorian public house (with its elaborate capitals still visible) and now a thriving youth club. When the pub closed in the 1970s, it was taken over by a group of local activists, including Graham Good and Peter Mandelson, later a Cabinet minister, and turned into The Winch, a club for disadvantaged locals. A fundraising campaign to upgrade the premises is currently raging. Below the Winch is the entrance to the new Swiss Cottage Leisure Centre (p 39). The southern stretch of Winchester Road combines the new **Swiss Cottage Community Centre**, opened in 2004 with upgraded facilities and a convenient café, and the **Visage**, a towering modern block of luxury apartments. Immediately to your left, useful shops have recently (2008) been flattened to make way for further luxury developments.

We turn and walk north to **ETON AVENUE**, briefly called Bursars Road, largely built up by William Willett between 1886 and 1894. At its western end, to our left, the road was at first blocked by the old School for the Blind, which for many years occupied No.100 Avenue Road. Willett bought out the school for £15,000, and from 1887 had access to Finchley Road – an arrangement which lasted until the 1960s, when the road was blocked up again.

Walk for a short distance to the right, into the Avenue. Three houses along is the first of the 16 Listed houses in this road, **No. 69**, North House, built in 1890 for the portrait painter John Collier, who successively married two daughters of the great Thomas Huxley. This high-flown mansion with elaborate staircase windows was designed in Flemish Renaissance style by Frederick Waller, the husband of yet another of Huxley's daughters. Terracotta plaques show the initials of John and Ethel Collier, and the date of the house. **No.58** (opposite) has a fine dragon up top. **No.57**, which houses a seminary, the Trevor Roberts Tutorial School, sports a dragon guarding a shield on the near corner and a pretty conservatory on the far one.

Retracing our steps towards the triangular open space (often filled with market stalls), we see to our left the **Hampstead Theatre** built by Bennetts Associates in 2003. Across the road, where the old Embassy Theatre and the new **Central School of Speech and Drama** now stand, there once flourished the Hampstead Conservatoire of Music and School of Art. Much of the original building of 1888, designed by Rowland Plumbe, is still visible. The Conservatoire prospered under the direction of the folk music enthusiast Cecil Sharp in the 1890s, but in the 1920s a decline set in, leading to the phoenix birth of the Embassy in 1929. The Central School finally took over in 1956.

Now much enlarged, with a brick modernist extension (1997) by Cullum & Nightingale, the school is part of the University of London.

Turn right and take the left-hand fork into **ADAMSON ROAD**, reputedly named after one of the Eton Estate contractors. This was completed by the mid-1880s. Most of the tall, rather severe houses, half of which were by William Willett, have survived. **Nos.2-6**, much whitened and beflagged, have become the handsome Swiss Cottage Hotel. A number of artists were living in this road in the early 1920s, notably Robert Bevan at **No.14** (recently plaqued). His studio had originally belonged to the landscape artist (Sir) Alfred East: the studio window is still there. Bevan, who was a founder member of Sickert's Camden Town Group, lived here from 1900 to his death in 1925. He painted many local street scenes **[13]** (see also front cover), and his work is well represented at Tate Britain, as is that of his wife, Stanislawa de Karlowska.

Adamson Road leads into largely yellow-brick **CROSSFIELD ROAD**, possibly commemorating another Eton contractor. Immediately across it is **The Hall School** at No.23, built in best red-brick Adam style by E R Robson in 1890. The Hall was originally a girls' school under the Misses

13 *From the Artist's Window* [at No.14 Adamson Road], Robert Bevan 1915, with Embassy Theatre to the left of No.3

Allen-Olney (p 54), and their initials are in the brickwork beside the front door. But in 1905 it was bought by the Belsize School for Boys. The remaining girls were first relegated to the Belsize School building in Buckland Crescent (p 51), and then eliminated altogether. As a boys' school, The Hall continued to flourish in both buildings, and in 1916 moved its Buckland Crescent branch as a junior school along to the corner of Belsize Park. In 1989 the school celebrated its centenary by publishing its history and building a yellow-brick extension to designs by Michael Haskoll Associates, "suited to young people in the 21st century". Across the road, a further bold extension, a red-brick-and-glass building with tall towers (numbered as **34 Eton Avenue**) designed by Shepperd Robson was added in 1997; this is the Middle School. Old Boys of The Hall, known as Old Aularians, include Clement Freud, John Schlesinger and Peter Shaffer.

The discovery in 1890 of a murder victim in Crossfield Road considerably upset the local residents and the fledgling school. The police soon apprehended the criminal, known as Mrs Pearcey (further grisly details in *Streets of Gospel Oak and West Kentish Town*) but the residents launched a petition to change the street name in view of the "recent tragic event". They were supported by the architect of a local building project, who complained to the Vestry that the crime tended to depreciate the value of his property. However, the protests were in vain, and for years the Misses Allen-Olney carefully used the postal address *The Hall, Hampstead*, shunning the name of Crossfield Road.

Follow the yellow-brick road northwards and turn right into Lancaster Grove (p 51) and right again into **STRATHRAY GARDENS**. Relatively little is known of this street, except that the name was approved in 1882, and that parts of the road were built in 1885-86 by Willett, which explains their grandeur. Willett's architect, Harry Measures, again produced, according to Andrew Saint, "an endlessly inventive galaxy of gables and bays, gryphons and baubles, and decorated gateposts". **No.2** has a fine example of a lightning conductor with sunflower. Gryphons or dragons can be seen on **Nos.4** and **7** and on **No.10**, which also has an attractive modern conservatory. The Russian singer Valentina Aksarova-Sturtz (1894-1959), who lived at **No.6** and died at No.10, has a striking tombstone in the parish churchyard (see *Buried in Hampstead*). **Hereward House School** at **No.14** has lost its dragon but kept its decorative doorway. **No.11** is a modern oddity but in matching red brick. On the corner with Eton Avenue is a handsome 1930s block of flats, **Eton Court**, with boldly columned balconies.

Back in **ETON AVENUE**, turn left but drink in the view on both sides of the road. Most of the grandiose houses in Eton Avenue repay inspection, inventive in design and replete with interesting decoration as they are. Across the road, **Nos. 37-39** and **31-33** are Willett-built to designs by the locally active Amos Faulkner. Pevsner (1952) commends these and other houses in the avenue by Harry Measures, and also those in the "Ernest Newton style, that is, less urban, more horizontal, with tile-hung gables and freely Georgian porches". **No.35** bears its date (1895) in its painted blue-and-white frieze together with what appear to be pineapples in hammocks and some diminutive urns, and on its side entrance in Merton Rise its original name, Villa Henriette. Decorations on the houses opposite include a small dragon or gryphon way up on **No.42,** rampant dogs carved on the porch of **No.36**, once the home of singer Walter Widdop, and vinous bargeboards over the door and principal window of Tudorish **No.30**.

No.15, Sarum Hall School, a preparatory school for girls previously at No.51, was built in 1995 on the site of an old people's home, demolished despite much local protest. The new building was designed by Allies & Morrison and won awards from both the Civic Trust and the RIBA.

Across the road, gems of Willett houses **Nos.22-32** are particularly worth looking at, as are **Nos.10-14**. Finally, **No.1** on the corner, with a Batterbury & Huxley look, has the initials of its first occupant, William Coode Adams, a doctor.

Now turn right into **PRIMROSE HILL ROAD**. The houses standing tall across the road, **Nos.48-44**, are the only original ones left in this street.

On the corner of the eastward stretch of **FELLOWS ROAD**, into which we turn left, is the **Hampstead Britannia Hotel**. This has grown considerably from the Clive Private Guest House, which opened its doors in Edwardian times and has been much rebuilt since. Further east is **No.2**, Seaford Lodge (now a guest house), which has a splendid display of Corinthian pilasters and decorative windows. This was the home from about 1870 until his death in 1911 of Sir Henry Harben **[14]**, a great champion of Hampstead causes. For many years active on the Vestry, he rose to become the first Mayor of Hampstead. Much of the money he made as President of the Prudential Assurance Company he passed on to local charities including libraries, churches, hospitals, schools, Fortune Green, Golders Hill Park and Parliament Hill Fields. His daughter inherited some of his fortune and his generosity, and is commemorated in **Mary Wharrie House**, one of the Council blocks nearby designed by D H McMorran and built between 1954 and 1976 (see also p 12). Another block, **Hancock Nunn House**, salutes a local pioneer in social service work (see *The Streets of Hampstead*). This group of Council housing is called the **Fellows Road Estate.** For many years **Nos.11-13** formed the Greenway Nursing Home and the last

14 Sir Henry Harben (1823-1911), who lived in Fellows Road

address of, among others, Enid Blyton, Nigel Balchin and Stephen Potter. **No.5** was the home of art historian (Sir) John Rothenstein from 1938, when he became director of the Tate Gallery. The artist Stanley Spencer was a frequent visitor. At the eastern end of Fellows Road is a small network of roads, taking their names from Eton College and among the first to be laid out on the Eton Estate. Under the careful watch of the college's surveyor, John Shaw, the roads were developed from the 1840s by Samuel Cuming, who was also responsible for most of Adelaide Road.

Turn left into **ETON ROAD,** until 1865 named Church Road, since plans for its church began in 1846 when a local surgeon, Henry Bird, called a meeting at the Load of Hay in Haverstock Hill to promote it. **St Saviour's,** finished in 1856, was designed by E M Barry, son of Sir Charles, and later architect of the Royal Opera House, Covent Garden. The handsome tower was added in 1864. Described by Cherry & Pevsner as "plain and old-fashioned for its date", the Grade-II-Listed building is embellished with fine carvings (especially the reredos) by Thomas Earp, who was also responsible for the Eleanor Cross designed by Barry at Charing Cross. Two octagonal brick buildings in the churchyard house the **vicarage** and **church hall**, ingeniously planned by David Martin in 1972. The church currently shares a vicar with St Peter's, Belsize Square.

On our left, almost opposite St Saviour's, is the **South Hampstead United Synagogue** by H J Georghiou, consecrated in 1962, which replaced the Regent's Park and Belsize Synagogue formerly in Eton Villas (see below). A further move (south) to Adelaide Road is planned (see p 32). The present block called **Wellington House** succeeded a large residence of the same name, designed and partly built for himself by Alfred Stevens (see below), and later occupied by the North London High School for Boys. A panelled and carved room was removed from this house to the Geffrye Museum in Shoreditch. **No.2**, on the right just before Haverstock Hill, was for many years the home of R D Laing, the controversial psychiatrist, author of *The Divided Self* (1960) which argued that "it could be society (aided by families and even psychiatrists) that was driving people mad". The house had earlier been the home of the vicar of St Saviour's, who was a well-known exorcist; this gave it the reputation of being haunted.

Return to the crossing with **ETON VILLAS** and turn right to view **No.18**, where Pietro Annigoni, famously portraitist of the Queen, lived from 1958 to 1961. All the semi-detached, 'Italian rustic' houses in Eton Villas, **Nos.1-20**, are Listed and are said to have been designed by John Shaw. Eton Villas has housed many artists over the years. A blue plaque on **No.9** on the southern arm proclaims the residence there of the artist Alfred Stevens from 1859 until his death in 1875. Son of a house painter, he rose to fame as a decorator of a higher calibre; his work includes a mosaic on the dome of St Paul's. He is best remembered now by his Wellington Monument in St Paul's, on which he worked inconclusively for his last 17 years. The architect of the National Portrait Gallery, Ewan Christian, lived at **No.6** Eton Villas in the 1850s: he later built himself a mansion in Well Walk (see *The Streets of Hampstead*). **No.1** was the home of the architectural historian Sir John Summerson until his death in 1992.

Eton Villas ends in **PROVOST ROAD**, also built in 1844; the Provost is the head of Eton College's governing body. It contains handsome **Nos.1-20**, with attractive period touches, all by John Shaw except perhaps No.20, a grey Gothic stucco villa at the west end. **No.14** was the home for many years of the popular thriller writer Gavin Lyall.

Turning left along Provost Road we reach **ETON COLLEGE ROAD**. This was known merely as College Road until 1936, and it seems to have been in existence for nearly 90 years by then. By 1888 there were still only two houses facing the street, all the others looking on to Eton Villas or Haverstock Hill. The massive apartment buildings **Eton Place** and **Eton Rise** were built in the late 1930s and **Eton Hall** in the late 1940s. Amongst recent flat-dwellers was the harmonica virtuoso Larry Adler. **No.2** and **No.3** Eton College Road are Listed buildings. James Cameron, the globe-trotting, trouble-shooting journalist, lived at No. 3: "he was", said his friend Michael Foot, "truly the prince of journalists".

At the bottom of Eton College Road is Adelaide Road, where buses can be caught. Or turn left to reach Chalk Farm Underground Station.

Route 6

Central Belsize

Circular walk from Haverstock Hill

This area is haunted by reminders of Belsize House and its extensive parkland. Belsize Lane, where we begin, ran outside the boundary, while the wide road which seems to provide an intended east-west through road is not, historically, one road but two. It began as Belsize Avenue, the main avenue leading to Belsize House from the King's Highway or Haverstock Hill, but was joined much later by a road beginning at College Crescent and dubbed, to the confusion of many to this day, Belsize Park. The two roads meet in a seamless junction at a crossroads where Belsize Park Gardens (p 53) zooms off southwards and Belsize Terrace (p 48) fans out to the north. These historical facts explain the unusual numbering of the houses in the two arms of the 'through road': the numbers in Belsize Avenue run eastwards from the crossroads, while those of Belsize Park begin at the top of Lancaster Grove and run sequentially eastwards to No.17 on the south side, returning westwards, starting from the crossroads, with No.18 on the north.

Our walk starts at the junction of Haverstock Hill with Belsize Lane, across the road from Hampstead Green. Most of the main streets in this section were laid out

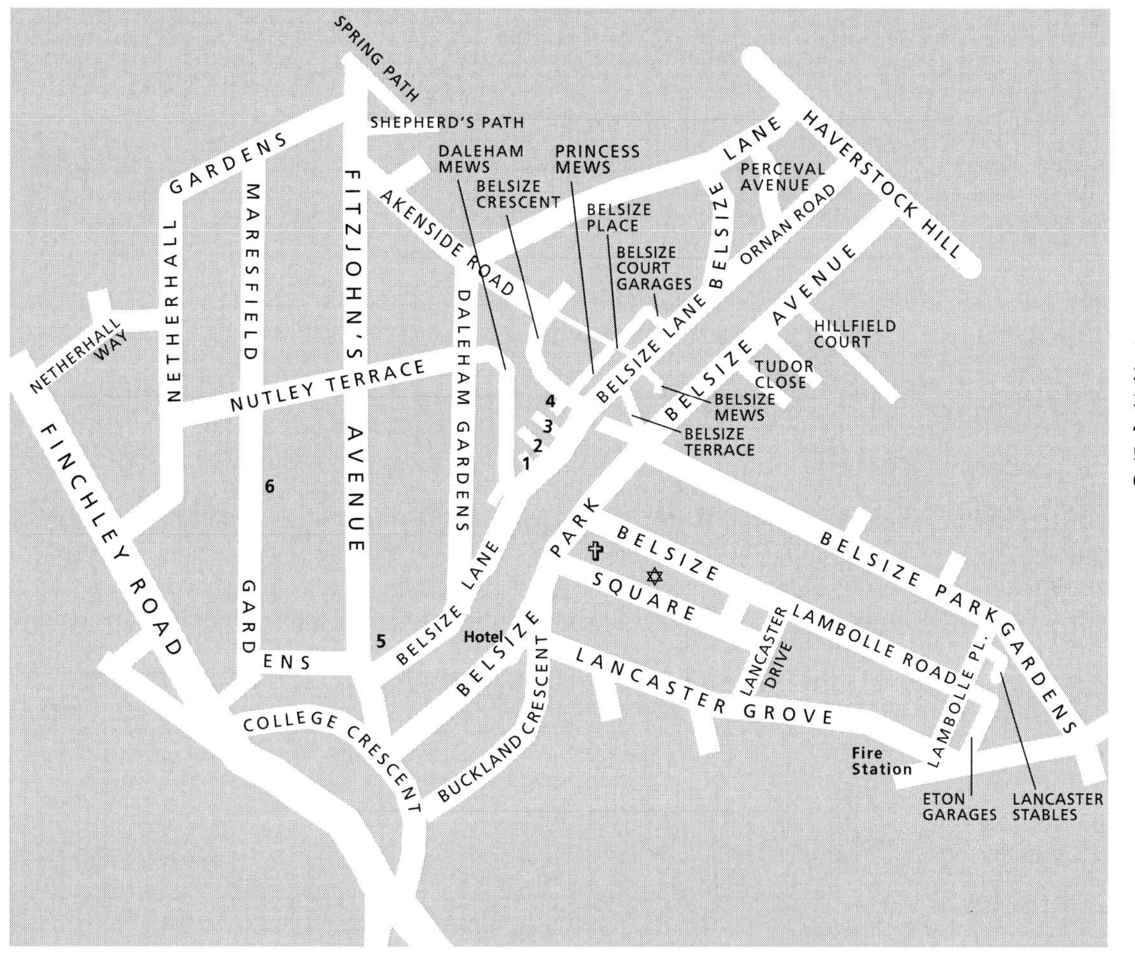

Map III

Central Belsize and Fitzjohn's

1 McCRONE MEWS
2 BAYNES MEWS
3 BELSIZE PARK MEWS
4 BURDETT MEWS
5 Tavistock Clinic
6 Freud Museum

at the same time – around 1860 – and have Belsize in their titles. For the origins of the name, see the Historical Overview (p 7); the impressive ring of 'Belsize' clearly had immense appeal through the ages and was much used in christening the roads and houses, so we are left with a confusion of names that may tire readers; the only consolation we can offer is that there are fewer Belsizes now than there once were.

BELSIZE LANE has the prime claim to the name. It is the oldest street in the area and it has some sharp curves. Old maps (for example, Faden 1788) suggest that this lane connected Hampstead's South End and West End but this is not so: the western stretch (farthest from us) was a private access road for Belsize Farm. The farm, about half-way along the present lane (which leads from the lower end of Fitzjohn's Avenue to Hampstead Green) on the northern side, was called Mr Thomas's Farm in the Vestry Minutes of 1864 and Belsize Farm on the 1866 OS map. The farmhouse was still standing about 1880, according to Walford. Adjoining the farm, near the lower entrance to Daleham Mews, was a toll gate, erected by the owner to show that the land was private. Tradition has it that Queen Victoria was halted at this gate on her way to inspect Rosslyn House as a summer holiday resort for her children. The toll-keeper's young daughter happened to be in charge, and very properly refused to let her pass without paying her penny. Contrary to form, the Queen *was* amused, and paid her toll.

Attempts were made in 1820 to widen Belsize Lane as part of a turnpike road from St Marylebone to Hampstead Green. The proposal was strongly resisted by local residents, who claimed it would damage and devalue their fine properties. Against this, evidence was given that the lane was ripe for redevelopment; the neighbourhood was run-down, the "resort of vagabonds" and full of "nuisances" for respectable ladies. Fortunately, as with so many Hampstead schemes, the protesters won.

Belsize Lane was greatly affected by the building boom of the early 1880s, when the whole of its eastern half, where we are now, was widened and tidied up. **Nos.2-26** were built at this time and called Rosslyn Gardens. It is known that No.2 was designed in 1883 by local architect Henry Spalding, and he was probably responsible for the whole development. The gateway to No.2 bears the name Rosslyn Heights, and an unexplained plaque says the house was opened by Sir Geoffrey Finsberg (then MP for Hampstead and Highgate) in 1987. On the opposite side, **Hunters Lodge [15]** fortunately survived the changes and remains the oldest and handsomest house in the street. Described by Pevsner as a "castellated Gothic house, exceedingly pretty in a toy way", this stuccoed and turreted *cottage orné* surprisingly has little history although, according to one legend, there was a hunting lodge on this site belonging to Queen Anne's husband, Prince George of Denmark. The present house was built soon after 1810 by a merchant, William Tate, who was among the petitioners in 1820 against the widening of the lane. Tate was a lessee of the Baltic merchant George Todd (see plaque in Hampstead Parish Church), who had acquired the lease of a large slice of Belsize Park in 1808. The architect of Hunters Lodge, then called Langwathby, was Joseph Parkinson, who exhibited the designs at the Royal Academy in 1810. For many years part of the Ivy Bank estate, the Lodge lost much of its grounds in the 1890s when Ornan Road was being built up. Cut down to its present size, the property became known as Belsize Cottage.

Turn left at the sharp bend in the Lane and look down the right-hand side at **St Christopher's Girls' School,** which has occupied **No.32** since 1919. The main building is curiously wrapped round a red-brick octagonal ventilator shaft of the second Belsize railway tunnel. The school grew up as a kindergarten in Carlingford Road, matured in Hampstead Hill Gardens, and finally flowered in Belsize Lane, after taking over two other local schools, Tremarth and Ruskin House. At the junction with Ornan Road is **No.19**, one of the Lane's many recycled coach houses.

Turn left along **ORNAN ROAD**, which

was named in 1873, but not built up until around 1890. The developer was Richard Pierce Barker, and the main contractor was a senior Vestryman, Richard Hackworth, of Loudoun Road. The street name remains inexplicable. **No.17A** and **No.40** are, says Pevsner, "austere but well-proportioned" houses by John Winter in 1970. **Nos.34-38** on the left as we approach Haverstock Hill are the few remaining original houses.

15 The Ivy Bank estate from Belsize Lane, with Hunters Lodge (left), early 19th century

Beyond them, **Ornan Court**, an early example of luxury flats, was built in 1893. A blue plaque (2003) salutes the master illusionist David Devant (famous for his Disappearing Donkey), who lived here in 1915-17. The building was bought in 2007 for development as a hostel with some underground rooms (despite local protest). The south side of the road is all modern, with **No.51** airing its date (1986) and some cherubs.

Return to the bottom of **PERCEVAL AVENUE**. There are no mysteries about its name. It commemorates the statesman Spencer Perceval, who married the younger daughter of Sir Thomas Wilson, Lord of the Manor of Hampstead, and who lived at Belsize House from 1798 to 1807. He moved from Lincoln's Inn Fields to this large, rambling mansion **[7]** with his thirteen children and little money. Fortunately, his legal and parliamentary career flourished and he rose to become Prime Minister. But little is remembered of his term of office except his sudden departure from it in 1812, when he was shot dead in the lobby of the House of Commons by a madman called John Bellingham. Perceval Avenue, once known as Beaulieu Avenue, was built across the grounds of Ivy Bank (p 47) in 1915.

Further west down **BELSIZE LANE** we see on the left several new houses built in the back gardens of Belsize Avenue, and on the right a long retaining wall behind which lurk **Nos.1-8 Village Close**. It is possible that the land on which they are built, which is several metres lower than present Lyndhurst Gardens, resulted from the digging out of the clay to make bricks for the 1496 Belsize House (p 7). Beyond **BELSIZE MEWS**, for long a garage complex which now accommodates twelve town houses, is **No.29**, a restaurant (in 2009) which used to be the Belsize Tavern, dating from the late 1850s and once known as the Henry VIII. Its first landlord was Daniel Tidey, who developed much of Belsize Park. Opposite is **BELSIZE PLACE**, connected with Akenside Road (p 61) by an old track, seen on the 1745 map, and still preserved as a narrow pathway. A large pond is shown here on Park's map of 1814, and the street name does not appear until 1886 (having previously been attached to the George Inn terrace in Haverstock Hill). The high wall flanking the path was evidently built in the 1880s, to retain the grounds of new houses in Lyndhurst Gardens. **BELSIZE COURT GARAGES** were built by William Willett as livery stables in 1880, but had no connection with the stately Belsize Court (p 69) up the hill. Many of the houses there still have hayloft doors, but only **No.2** has kept its hoist.

Here begins the so-called **Belsize Village**, which dates only from mid-Victorian times. **Nos.29-39 BELSIZE LANE** were originally built (in the late 1850s) as 1-6 Upper Belsize Terrace, and are followed without a break by present-day **Nos.7-12 BELSIZE TERRACE** (without the 'Upper') curving round to the south. Nos.1-6 were renumbered as part of Belsize Lane by the time of the 1921 Directory. Willett gave up land in order to open up the triangular Belsize 'village green', which has enough small shops to give a villagey feeling and is now smartly paved and furnished with benches and bollards. At the southern end, **No.12** (now a restaurant) began as the dairy shop of William Thomas of Belsize Farm. An advertisement of the time **[16]** showed that he kept Alderney cows for invalids, and was "a purveyor of goat's and asse's [sic] milk". The link across the terrace to Belsize Park Gardens (once a popular rat-run) was blocked in 1995, after much protest by businesses and shopkeepers, but ultimately proving advantageous to them. The terrace of shops along the north side of the triangle and straddling Belsize Crescent, **Nos.46-72 BELSIZE LANE,** was part of the first project by William Willett, Senior, in this area (see also Belsize Crescent, later). Willett seized his chance when the developer Daniel Tidey went bankrupt in 1869, and built what Prout called "standard speculator's Italianate" shops with flats above.

Leaving the 'village' behind, continue along **BELSIZE LANE** on its north side as far as Daleham Mews. The builders of the new district of Belsize Park aimed at carriage-conscious customers, and

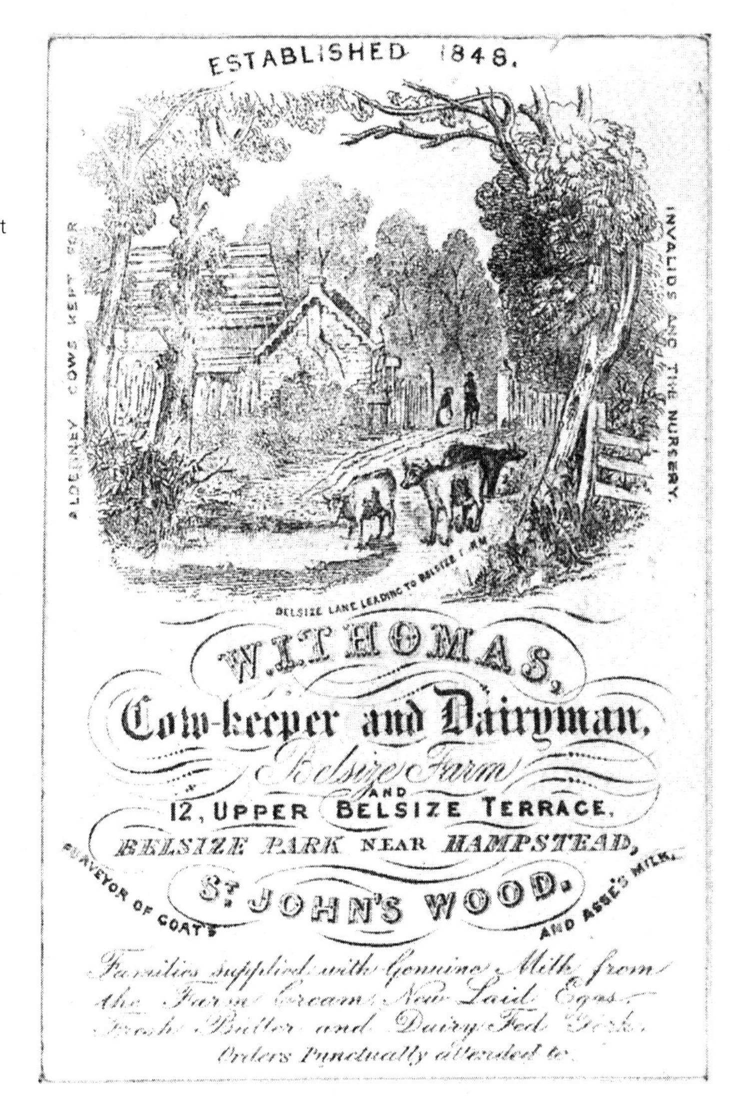

16 Advertisement for Belsize Farm dairyman at No.12 (then Upper) Belsize Terrace

therefore provided a fine collection of mews: these are now smart, domesticated backwaters. **DALEHAM MEWS** is the largest one, connecting up with Daleham Gardens (p 62). Turn back along the Lane and pass **McCRONE MEWS**, named after the firm which once occupied **No.2** (McCrone is a name well known in microscopy.) On the 1916 Ordnance Survey map, the Mews is shown as the London Parcel Delivery Company's Depot. An imposing arched entrance leads to the next inlet. **BAYNES MEWS** was built by William Willett around 1871, and appropriately called William's Mews, but now it commemorates an editor of the *Encyclopaedia Britannica* who lived locally. Lastly **BELSIZE PARK MEWS**, now converted into residences, buzzed with servicing industries in the 1920s, including a Canine and Feline Infirmary and a Bath Chair Proprietor.

At the corner turn left up **BELSIZE CRESCENT**, another early development of William Willett Senior, who had the name changed from Prince Consort Road in 1873. The style is "rather cramped Italianate", says Pevsner. **No.6** is noted in architectural circles as Willett Senior's first house in Hampstead: his style later became much more ambitious and decorative, more like **No.24**, designed by H B Measures in 1884 (see also Lyndhurst Gardens, p 69). With its ornate porch and pointed gate pillars, the house is now Grade-II Listed. Connoisseurs of boot scrapers will note sadly that few of Willett's originals have survived. Fashion fans will thrill to hear that Lesley Hornby, alias Twiggy, lived at **No.20** before she budded out as top model in the Swinging Sixties. **No.13** was for many years the home of composer and conductor Berthold Goldschmidt, who died here in 1996. His expertise on Gustav Mahler helped to complete Mahler's unfinished 10th Symphony in 1960. Before WWII, **No.4** was a knitting factory belonging to the London Society for Teaching and Training the Blind (p 39). Lovers of Sherlock Holmes will enjoy the useless information that in 1935 adjacent houses in the Crescent were occupied by Mrs Watson, Miss Baskerville and Mrs Moriarty.

17 Belsize House (engraving of 1845)

Returning from these delights down the hill, note two old mews at the southern end. **BURDETT MEWS** on the right salutes its long-term owner, William Burdett, who walked from Stamford in the 1850s to start a hacking business behind the Belsize Tavern, and later opened his carriage-making premises in the mews. His son and grandson continued the firm's operations, which inevitably turned into a garage. This has now become a small gated residential backwater. **PRINCESS MEWS** on the left, again built by William Willett, appears first in the Vestry Minutes of 1873 because of defective drains and suspected scarlet fever. The mews' name may commemorate Princess Louise, who married the Marquis of Lorne in 1871. The wedding caused a slight stir, as it was the first time that an English princess had married non-royalty since Mary Tudor, daughter of Henry VII, became the wife of the Earl of Suffolk in 1515. The mews has now also become residential.

Now cross to the point of the triangular 'village green'. Left of the mulberry tree on the corner lies Belsize Avenue (p 54), but we turn right along the road called **BELSIZE PARK**. Amid the confusion of Belsize titles, none has worked harder than this one. Originally a literal description of the 25-acre grounds of Belsize House **[17]**, the name is found on Weller's map of 1862 (**[8]**, p 25) applied to a short row of houses west of St Peter's Church. The 1873 Directory appears to use the name for the northern segment of the street only, and it is not until a decade later that the name is applied to the whole road. Walk along the north side, starting with No.18 on the right, with numbers increasing sequentially westwards all the way to the junction with College Crescent (p 55). Most of the original classical houses remain from the 1850s, which in their early days especially attracted the *nouveaux riches*, but some of "the white cliffs of Belsize" crumbled in later years.

No.9 on the south side was the home of Keith Vaughan, the figurative artist and Slade Professor, from 1952 until his death in 1977. Barratt records that **No.27** was the home of Sir Henry Isaacs, an eminent Fruit Broker, who was Lord Mayor of London in 1889-90. "A Jew of the purest type", said the *Hampstead Yearbook*, "he is only the third man of that creed to occupy the civic throne". His son Rufus (1860-1935) was such a wild youth that he was dubbed "the rake of Belsize Park". But he became a brilliant barrister and successively Lord Chief Justice, Viceroy of India and, as

Lord Reading, Foreign Secretary. No.27 was bought in 1919 by Kingsley School, as was **No.26** in 1923, and the pair became the Junior School and boarding house, while **No.46** became the Senior School and staff accommodation. The most famous of the school's principals was Lizzie Susan Stebbing, who was also Professor of Philosophy at London University. Kingsley was the only school in England to offer Logic at School Certificate level, the classes being taught by Miss Stebbing, who was also President of the Aristotelian Society and of the Mind Association – as well as author of the best-selling *Thinking to Some Purpose*. The school was evacuated during WWII and never returned. After the war, No.27 became first a youth hostel and then a boys' club for Holocaust survivors.

The eccentric Mrs Violet van der Elst lived at **No.30** for many years. A washerwoman's daughter, she first married Henry Nathan of No.80 Belsize Park Gardens (p 53), and in 1912 moved with him into this house in Belsize Park. Here she turned the kitchen into a face-cream factory, and concocted Doge Cream, "based on an old Venetian recipe". From this, and the first brushless shaving cream, she made a fortune. When her husband died mysteriously in 1927, she married their lodger, John van der Elst, and moved to Kensington. Soon after her second husband's death in 1934, she launched her dramatic campaign for the abolition of capital punishment, and for 25 years appeared outside every prison where an execution was imminent.

The distinctly 1950s style of **No.35** and **No.36** (architects Charles Box and Frank Scarlett respectively) betrays where a bomb fell in the last war. **No.41** was Jerome K Jerome's last home. He started as a clerk at Euston Station, achieved fame with *Three Men in a Boat* and *The Passing of the Third Floor Back*, and in 1924, at the height of his fame, moved into Belsize Park, clearly a success symbol at the time. He also came here from the depths of Buckinghamshire on medical advice, because long walks and other country pursuits were said to be bad for his health. He died three years later. **Nos.46** is the old-established Avoca House Hotel. **No.69**, which has been part of The Hall School since 1916 and currently functions as the Junior School, was immortalised in a painting by Robert Bevan in 1917 (see cover).

BUCKLAND CRESCENT's name commemorates Dean Buckland (1784-1856) of Westminster Abbey. After early references to Buckland Road and Buckland Villas (1856), the present name was approved in 1861. The street appears fully built up (mostly by Daniel Tidey) on the 1866 OS map. Little has been recorded about the residents here except by the redoubtable Elizabeth Garrett Anderson, who visited her future in-laws at **No.7** on the eve of her marriage in 1871. **No.15A** was for many years (until 2008) the home of Lady Evelyn Barbirolli, leading oboist and widow of the conductor and cellist Sir John. It was here she created a famously beautiful garden, which she opened annually to the public. **No.18** was the first home of The Hall School (see p 41) and became a girls' school in 1905. In the 1920s, **No.27** was the base of (Sir) Alan Cobham, the pioneer of long-distance flying, and vigorous propagandist of British aviation. His trailblazing flights to Cape Town and Australia in 1926 caused an international sensation. The noted photographer Edwin Smith lived at **No.29** for many years. **No.45** has a decorative gate leading to the Eton Montessori Nursery.

Almost opposite The Hall Junior School, turn down **LANCASTER GROVE**, which is said to be named after Edmund, Earl of Lancaster (1245-96), second son of Henry III, though the connection seems tenuous (might it, rather, refer to Henry VI, Duke of Lancaster, already mentioned as founder of Eton College?). The road was developed from this north-western end about 1866 and was known as Lancaster Road until 1936. **Nos.1** and **3** are post-bombing replacement blocks. The semi-stuccoed **Nos.9-35** were the first to be built in Belsize style, but some of their porches have been downgraded. **No.37**, still called Thornton, was erected by John Galloway in 1881 and shows a change in style to solid red brick with decorative bargeboards. Overgrown

18 Lancaster Grove from the south-east (end of Lambolle Place to the right) Edwardian postcard

No.20 across the road was the home of the drama director Dr Martin Browne, who died there in 1980. Apart from local music and theatre, he was famously associated with religious and poetic drama, notably the plays of T S Eliot. **No.45** is dated 1885 on a plaque, while **No.69** has 1891 over its door, shortly before the junction with Lambolle Place (p 53) **[18]**. The only Listed building is across the road, the **fire station** designed by C C Winmill and built in 1915, on a site originally reserved by the Eton Estate for a church. There was a saw-mill here in the 1890s. The impressive building, which includes garages and firemen's quarters, is praised by Pevsner for its "powerful brick hose-and-water tower" and for its "well-handled detail in the free vernacular".

Return past large houses (including No.20) set well back from and rather lower than the road level, and turn right into **LANCASTER DRIVE**, which was built by John Galloway in the 1880s, although in this first stretch we see only infilling modern **No.9**. Further along, we encounter the curious phenomenon of a street built one side in classical white and cream stucco and the other in red brick with white trim – odd numbers on one side, even numbers on the other, equal in height but utterly disparate in character and size of front garden. Ignoring this curiosity, take the first turn left, which forms one side of **BELSIZE SQUARE**. The Square was referred to in the Vestry Minutes of 1863 as St Peter's Road (North and South), but it was given its present name on the 1866 OS map.

The classical houses on the left are numbered from 26 to 1 (at the top end, by the church). Former residents include Patrick Caulfield, the painter and printmaker, at **No.19**, and John Drinkwater at **No.10** in 1921-22. On the right, we pass, first, a Jewish community hall (built 1973) and then the Belsize Square Synagogue (see later), closely followed by **St Peter's Church**, which was erected by J P St Aubyn and W Mumford in 1859; it was one of a dozen new churches opened in Hampstead in a mere 25 years. The building is noted by Pevsner as of "earnest ragstone" with "spiky gables over the nave windows". Being built on land given by the Dean of Westminster, who added a small endowment, it was not surprisingly named after the Abbey of St Peter, Westminster. (The Dean and Chapter are still patrons of the living.) Another benefactor was the first vicar, Rev. Dr F W Tremlett, who paid for the nave, aisles and transepts, while his parishioners took care of the chancel. The eccentric Dr Tremlett was vicar here for over half a century, and there is a portrait bust of him by Kathleen Shaw (1915) in the church. He was a fanatical champion of the southerners in the American Civil War. When the Alabama, a Confederate vessel, was sunk off Cherbourg by a Federal ship in 1864, Dr Tremlett found accommodation locally for the rescued admiral and officers.

The original vicarage for St Peter's was built in 1861 at its eastern end. This was replaced in 1917 by a grand Tudorish brick house, which in 1947 was sold to the **Belsize Square Synagogue**, which first renovated the old vicarage, and then in 1958 built a new synagogue using the Bauhaus-trained architect H W Reifenberg. A reminder of the proximity of the river Tyburn is provided by the need to pump out the basement of the synagogue, which floods after rain: an electric pump installed for this purpose is frequently in use.

The current **vicarage** adjoins St Peter's on the north side; it was completed in 1953. The church was prominent in the 1990s for embracing the ordination of women and for continuing its strong friendship with the synagogue next door. There is at present also a link with the Ethiopian Orthodox Church. The vicar is also in charge of St Saviour's, Eton Road.

Now walk down the north side of the Square (numbered 50-31). Here lived Hugo Manning, the poet, at **No.46**, where he is commemorated by a private plaque; Ronald Fraser, the actor and bon viveur at **No.40**; the artist Frank Budgen at **No.39**; and the actor Miles Malleson at **No.27**, one of the curiously numbered houses in the short cross-piece that completes the Square.

After No.31 the north side of Belsize Square runs into **LAMBOLLE ROAD**. Many of the houses on its south side were built by John Galloway. The street name was approved in 1876 but never explained. The name was requested by Mr S G Bird, the builder of many local houses, and owner of brick-kilns behind Belsize Park Gardens, which much offended the proud noses of local residents in 1873. **No.14** on the left was the home of the eminent philosopher Professor John Findlay, author and lecturer, and a leading light of the Aristotelian Society (see p 51). In the early 1900s, the Aumonier family living at **No.40** included the sculptor William and his more famous son Stacey, a popular short-story writer. Journalist and broadcaster Brian Inglis lived at **No.23** from 1972 to 1993.

LAMBOLLE PLACE at the bottom, originally an extension of Lancaster Grove, was officially renamed in 1897. Together with the adjoining **ETON GARAGES** and **LANCASTER STABLES** (recently changed from Lancaster Garages) the buildings buzz with a hive of small industry, mostly motor repairs. A turn left will bring you in a short distance to Belsize Park Gardens. **No.24 LAMBOLLE PLACE** on the right-hand corner is now part of the Hampstead Fine Arts College.

The neighbouring house in **BELSIZE PARK GARDENS, No.81**, for long the Hampstead Squash and Fives Club, continues to promote fitness as Spring Health & Leisure Club. Next door to it are four Willett houses, **Nos.83-89**, built in 1896. This is where the Belsize Estate ends and the Eton Estate begins. Backtrack up Belsize Park Gardens, which Pevsner found "most impressive ... a grandiose and relentless march of massive paired palazzi with Ionic porches and robust vermiculated quoins". The road runs parallel to a notorious path round the north-east walls of the Belsize House grounds, once known as 'Cut-throat Alley'. The track is shown on the 1745 map, and it was here exactly 100 years later that a Hampstead man, James Delarue, was robbed and stabbed by Thomas Hocker, a music teacher of St John's Wood. "One of the worst murders I ever read of", wrote Charles Dickens to a friend, much regretting that it was "in one of my daily walks near Hampstead". Hocker was quickly caught and hanged. Soon after the murder, Belsize House came down, and the present rows of near-identical town houses went up. The north-western end of the road, which we shall presently reach, first appears on the 1862 map, and was originally St Margaret's Road (presumably after St Margaret's, Westminster). The present name was approved in 1885.

Lytton Strachey reluctantly stayed at two different houses in Belsize Park Gardens, which became his family homes. In 1907 the Stracheys moved to the then dilapidated **No.67**, where Lytton had his own bed-sitter and wrote his *Spectator* reviews. He had friends at hand, such as Henry Lamb in the Vale of Health, where Lamb painted the famous Strachey portrait, and his cousin Duncan Grant in Fellows

Road, with whom he would "walk on the Heath and catch 'flu together". But his letters refer to the "ghastly solitude" of Belsize Park Gardens, and in one such fit of depression he even proposed to Virginia Woolf. The year WWI broke out, the family moved northwards to **No.6** and it was there that Strachey wrote much of his *Eminent Victorians*. No.6 was earlier the home of marine artist Clarkson Stanfield, who came from Stanfield House in Hampstead High Street (see *The Streets of Hampstead*) in 1865, and died here two years later.

No.53 was the home of Tom Eckersley, the masterly poster artist (e.g. for London Transport): he died here in 1997. **No.41** had become a "select school for young ladies" by 1889, under the Misses Allen-Olney, formerly headmistresses of Blackheath and South Hampstead High Schools respectively. So successful was it that they built The Hall in Crossfield Road (p 41). **No.44** has a blue plaque to the composer Frederick Delius, who lived here in 1918-19 at the height of his career. The New Zealand artist Frances Hodgkins, "a notable colourist" (DNB), lived at **No.40** in 1932: this now belongs to the London Hostels Association.

No.37 bears a blue plaque to the influential Socialist journalist H N Brailsford, "champion of equal and free humanity", who died here in 1958. In the 1930s, this was the home of Jack Pritchard, art-loving industrialist, who founded the Isokon furniture firm (see p 24) and gave shelter to artists such as Mondrian (see p 29).

When the Belsize Estate was being sold by Westminster in the 1850s, *The Illustrated London News* predicted that it would soon be "converted into a London suburban-villa district with its fine modern church, its pretentious tavern and all those other parasitical edifices which grow up so rapidly". They were right about the church but, for the rest, Belsize Park became a respectable and desirable residential district and did not lose its dignity.

Of course, not all the inhabitants of Belsize Park Gardens were rich and famous; many must have been the kind of mildly prosperous, respectable folk represented by the fictional Rudolf Rassendyll's solicitor, who is pictured opening a letter at his home in Belsize Park Gardens (number unspecified!) on the first page of Anthony Hope's 1894 novel *The Prisoner of Zenda*.

No.2 has a curious claim to fame, being the address on the very first parcel delivered by the Post Office in August 1883. The package had been dispatched by local historian F E Baines, who was in charge of the new postal service, and had only travelled from Haverstock Hill: there is no record of how long it took to arrive. Jumping a century, the steel and glass packages at **No.2C** and **No.2D** are two well-hidden houses built for themselves by architects Spencer & Webster in 1981: they are described by admirers as "minimalist architecture at its most positive".

A little beyond **No.2A**, The Coach House, we turn right into **BELSIZE AVENUE**, which stretches north-eastwards, eventually climbing to Haverstock Hill. This was originally the carriage drive to Belsize House and can be recognised as such on the Rocque map of 1745, but it was not built up until the 1850s. Even then it remained a private road for some years, with a five-barred gate at the Haverstock Hill end until 1855. **No.1**, across the road from where we stand, next to the mulberry tree, has composed a charming garden in the hollow trunk of another old (but dead) tree of the Belsize House estate. The mulberry tree is a survivor from the garden of Belsize House. This and another mulberry behind No.26 Belsize Park (to the left) marked the corner of the grounds.

Building in the avenue was originally controlled very strictly by the Dean and Chapter of Westminster: when the Woodds bought the land in the 1850s, they had to agree not to "erect any House of a less class of Building than those erected [already]... nor erect houses nearer than 50 feet from the centre of the Avenue Road, nor diminish the width of the road near the two bridges", which accounts for the very wide verges still extant in front of the front gardens. No bridges appear on any maps of the time, but they probably crossed culverts carrying part of the Tyburn river, which rises near here (see also p 56). Westminster Abbey was also instrumental in preserving the avenue's stately trees. A condition of their sale of land in 1887 was that Hampstead Vestry should replace any dead trees. The present Cornish elms are at least 50 years old.

As you walk up the left-hand pavement from No.1 notice **No.11**, where a future Japanese Prime Minister, Takeo Fukuda, lived in the 1930s, when working at the Japanese Embassy. There is a remarkable range of Willett ornamentation on most of the houses between **No.25** and **No.51,** built around 1873. Notable residents of the avenue have included film star Gordon Harker at **No.45** and at **No.37** Reina Lawrence, the first woman in the country to be elected a Borough Councillor. She stood for Belsize ward in 1907, saying "I am not an agitator for women's rights...I do not intend to introduce sex problems in Council discussions". **Nos.53-59** are replacements built in the 1990s in a similar style.

Across the way, the two parallel enclosures of **Tudor Close** were also built in the 1930s, ousting some popular tennis courts used by, among others, the Mitsubishi Tennis Club. The flats, a triumph of Tudoresque architecture, have blocks named after Cranmer, Latimer and other top people of the period.

Most of the houses on the southern side of **BELSIZE AVENUE** are worth a glance – **Nos.44-60** for the oriels by their front doors, **Nos.18-28** for their terracotta flora. **No.56** was the home of the architect and town planner Sir James Stirling in the 1980s: his Clore Gallery at what is now Tate Britain was opened in 1987. **No.30**, Howard House, is a young people's hostel, now run by St Christopher's Fellowship (no connection with the girls' school in Belsize Lane).

The gate at Haverstock Hill was demolished in 1855 and the entrance to the avenue was rebuilt in 1871-72, with retaining walls and railings on the present lines, and much planting of shrubs. Part of the cost was met by Basil Woodd, whose land abutted on the avenue. Some of it was taken for two extensions to the Town Hall, in 1885 and in 1911, the latter proudly displaying the Hampstead Borough Arms. The total size of Woodd's property, Hillfield, can be judged from the vastness of the block of flats built on the site in the 1930s, **Hillfield Court**. Part of this area was Woodd's orchard, and some of his fruit trees have survived. In the garden a barrage balloon was moored in WWII. The beautiful actress Diana Wynyard lived at No.104 Hillfield Court just before her death in 1964. No.58 was for many years the home of German photographer Bill Brandt.

You have come full circle, back onto Haverstock Hill and its bus routes.

Route 7

The Fitzjohn's area

Circular walk from Swiss Cottage

For map see p 45

This walk begins and ends at Swiss Cottage, at the Underground station or at one of the many bus stops nearby. We start walking towards Hampstead up **COLLEGE CRESCENT**. This College refers not to Eton but to a short-lived theological training establishment for non-conformists. This was the imposing New College that was built together with much of the Crescent in 1851, but in 1934 pulled down in favour of the flat-lands of the present **Northways** on the left. (A newer New College was established at No.527 Finchley Road.) Some of Northways was taken over by the Navy in WWII for submarine control headquarters. College Crescent was originally the name of a single terrace of houses at this southern end, now demolished, while the next houses on either side of the road 'Belsize Park' were jointly called College Terrace. The 1896 Ordnance Survey map shows the western leg of the Crescent curving round and steeply down to Finchley Road as College Villas Road, but all this confusion ended in 1909, when the present name was approved for the whole road.

We first encounter **Nos.16-24**, which have laudably kept their decorative balconies.

No.25 has an eye-catching veranda. **No.26** was an early home of Nigel Kennedy, the tabloid-titled 'punk violinist'. Across the road, imposing **No.40** was, at the turn of the 20th century, the home of Samuel Palmer, of Huntley & Palmer's biscuits; his family presented the elaborate drinking fountain at the corner with Fitzjohn's Avenue in his memory in 1904. This has a plaque to the Palmers and another to the Heath and Old Hampstead Society, who in 1994 raised funds to restore the structure – now more of a flower stall than a fountain. No.40, built in 1881 and a Listed building, was donated by Palmer for hospital usage, and this continued until 1995. It has recently become a hostel for 'boutique backpackers' or 'budget travellers' and is called Palmers Lodge. Further on to the left, **No.36** has recently become the **Phoenix School**, part of the UCS group.

At the fountain we meet the most important road in our survey, **FITZJOHN'S AVENUE.** Its development and that of the surrounding area had long been planned by the Maryon-Wilson family, the Lords of the Manor of Hampstead, but it was not until 1869 that this became legally possible. The announcement that much rich agricultural land would be lost naturally caused an outcry from contemporary conservationists, notably from Octavia Hill. "How fresh the air blew over these fields", she wrote in the *Ham and High*, "and what fine views their hilly slopes commanded". She also threw herself into a fund-raising campaign to save the fields, and reportedly came within £1,000 of her target.

Other objectors stressed the area's literary connections. Was not this the sacred spot where Shelley rambled with Keats in "the beautiful meadows of Shepherd's Fields"? Had not Leigh Hunt written sonnets about these serene southern slopes? But serenity was no salvation. In 1875 the 50 acres of land were sold to developers for £50,000 (a fraction of the current price of a single bed-sit here now), and the avenue was named after a Maryon Wilson estate in Essex. (There is no apostrophe in the original place-name, but popular usage has introduced one.)

The new road followed an old footpath linking St John's Wood with Hampstead. "There are residents still", wrote Anna Maxwell in 1910, "who once walked up the steep, narrow path, climbing over the stiles to the top of the Conduit Fields... What matter that vandalistic hands have broadened the footway and named it Fitzjohn's Avenue. This is an innovation which we must severely ignore". The old path also led to the popular Shepherd's Well, now marked by a cream plaque at the forked junction with Akenside Road/ Lyndhurst Road. (The commemorative fountain mentioned on the plaque had suffered so much damage from hooligans that it was removed in 1988.) Shepherd's Well was the main source of the River Tyburn, which flows (now in conduits) to the Thames via the lake in Regent's Park and past Buckingham Palace. It was also Hampstead's main water supply, the purest of waters, which never froze in the hardest of winters. In the summer water carriers, who charged one penny per bucket, sometimes had to queue at the well for hours. With the coming of piped water (the reservoir in Hampstead Grove was built in 1856), the spring lost favour and, when the local land went up for sale, was described as "filthy and disreputable". The northern part of the new road followed a track from the well to Hampstead village. This avenue now swept into the heart of the village and brought about the Town Improvements of 1883-88, including the breakthrough into the High Street. (See *Streets of Hampstead*.)

Fitzjohn's Avenue was an immediate success. Barratt refers to "this commanding, tree-beautified avenue of stately dwellings", and others praised it as "tree-embowered" (the original pink chestnuts were later replaced with planes), and "one of the most beautiful avenues in the metropolis". The American magazine *Harpers* capped this in 1883 with "a long and stately avenue...one of the noblest streets in the world". It added: "The houses are all built in the fashion known as Queen Anne's." This so-called Queen Anne fashion was regretted by Gilbert Scott as a breakaway from his Gothic Revival, but today it is hard to see any style here except Victorian Eccentric. As Barratt also said, "the houses were considered very wonderful by a generation accustomed to the frowning dinginess of Georgian bricks and mortar". To ensure a prestigious neighbourhood, the Maryon Wilsons insisted in every building contract that no house "shall at any time be erected on the said piece of land of less value than £3,000".

Popular artists such as Frank Holl and John Pettie soon dominated the avenue, and when their houses were opened on 'Show Sunday' they attracted the smart set from all over London. "The Sunday parade", recalled Sir Max Pemberton (p 61), "should have been a source of inspiration and delight to the makers of fashion-plates". It also inspired Bernard Shaw to make a character in *Mrs Warren's Profession* claim that she learned about art from "some artistic people in Fitzjohn's Avenue".

At the foot of the hill (but beyond the present first building, the **Territorial Army Centre**), **No.1** was built by J J Stevenson, a pupil of Gilbert Scott, in 1883. The date and various mottoes appear on terracotta plaques on the entrance front on Maresfield Gardens, some of them clearly connected with the Oakwood Property Company, owned by Frank Debenham and (Sir) Edwin Lutyens. Debenham, the store magnate, was an early occupant of the house, and Lutyens was engaged in 1908 to make alterations, described as a "terraced shelter" not now detectable. From the 1950s this building (now Listed) belonged to the Territorial Army, but they sold it to the ever-expanding South Hampstead High School (p 59) and erected the above-mentioned Centre next door, designed by Monro & Partners.

No.3, across Maresfield Gardens, was the residence and studio of Philip de Laszlo from 1921 until his death in 1937 (see private plaque). Born in Budapest in 1869, de Laszlo became a fashionable portrait painter in London and many of his works are in the National Portrait Gallery. His house, along with **Nos.5&7**, are currently being redeveloped as flats with their original façades rebuilt. Laszlo's studio at the rear of No.3 was left to the church of St Thomas More in Maresfield Gardens (p 59) and currently functions as a Catholic Social Centre.

Across the Avenue, at the junction with Belsize Lane, sits **Sigmund Freud**, a bronze statue by Oscar Nemon (also responsible for Churchill in Parliament Square). Originally designed in Vienna in 1930, the statue was previously sited unhappily in Adelaide Road, but arrived here in 1997. At its unveiling, Jonathan Miller said it was lovely to see Freud "commanding the entrance to this avenue of the unconscious". Up the hill from it stretches the side of vast, stark **Tavistock Centre** for teaching and research in

19 Mission Hall, Belsize Lane (photograph 1875)

clinical, social and industrial psychology (for its front entrance see p 63).

Originally on its site a mission hall **[19]** was erected in 1865, chiefly aimed at the "local and licentious navvies" building the Midland Railway. Its first vicar, Henry Sharpe, fresh from the Canadian backwoods, would even go 60ft underground to preach the gospel to the diggers of the Belsize Tunnels. The mission attracted local residents, too, who eventually raised money to build Holy Trinity church in Finchley Road.

Further up Fitzjohn's Avenue, on the left-hand side, **No.11** is one of the B'nai B'rith Lodges, which aim to promote

Judaism and support charities. The Leo Baeck Hall at the rear was opened in 1980 (see also p 62). **No.15** was the birthplace of film director John Schlesinger in 1926. **No.27** was the home of Charles Hengler, the circus proprietor, until his death in 1887: his famous 'cirque' was on the site of the London Palladium. The novelist Rafael Sabatini lived at No.27 in the 1920s.

Many of the houses in Fitzjohn's Avenue had ceased to be private residences by the late 1930s, becoming guest houses, nursing homes or schools. Many have stayed that way. **No.33**, for instance, turned into the Eagle's Nest Foster Home around 1937 and is now the **North Bridge House Nursery School**. The building is one of several in this street that have the original frenzied façades, including ornamented eaves and decorative porches sporting sunflowers in carved brick. Beyond Nutley Terrace, **Southwell House, No.39** and its two neighbours are now a lively Youth Centre run by the Society of Jesus. **No.45**, though defiantly modernised, still bears its 1878 plaque, while **No.47**, built by George Lethbridge in 1880 (and now Listed), remains, according to Andrew Saint, "decent sub-Queen-Anne style" **[20]**. The original owner here was Louis Marino Casella, inventor of the clinical thermometer, whose family sold the house in 1927 to its present owners, St Mary's Convent School, formerly in England's Lane; the school also owns **No.49**.

20 *Beauchêne*, No.47 Fitzjohn's Avenue (Lethbridge, 1880)

In the 1890s another unsung hero of scientific invention lived at **No.51** (then called Lune Lea). This was James Mansergh (1834-1905), ingenious designer of sewage and waterworks, aqueducts and reservoirs in London, the Midlands and abroad. His neighbour at **No.53** was one David Landauer, whose initials appear on the doorway with the date 1897. But the date of the actual house was 1880, shown higher up. The Tower, **No.55**, a fine example of Disneyland Gothic (and now Listed), was designed by the Mayfair architect J T Wimperis in 1880 for Herbert Fleming Baxter. Now split up into apartments, the mansion still has Baxter's initial on its weathervane, along with a few other quirky original details.

At The Tower turn back down to Southwell House and turn right onto the western part of **NUTLEY TERRACE**. This was laid out, following the line of the old Belsize tunnel, on both sides of Fitzjohn's Avenue and named after another Maryon Wilson property in Sussex. Only a few houses were built on it in 1878 at the eastern end (p 62).

At the corner with **MARESFIELD GARDENS**, turn left to explore its southern stretch. The name commemorates another of the Maryon Wilson properties, a few miles from Nutley, in East Sussex. After a brief period as Maresfield Terrace, the present name was officially blessed in 1880. Odd numbers are on the right-hand side. On the left, **Nos.32-24**, dated 1884 and initialled JW (for Julius Wilson, their builder), display delightfully fanciful gables, some with pargetting. Among the earliest residents at **No.39** was Henry Moore RA, a once important marine painter, who died here in 1896, and at **No.31** Charles Mudie, founder in 1842 of the famous circulating library. The Liberal leader Herbert Asquith moved from Keats Grove to the newly-built **No.27** with his first wife Helen and family in 1887. When unveiling the black Hampstead plaque in 1983, a later Liberal leader, David Steel, commented that Asquith's five-year stay here "had seen the transformation of a rather dour lawyer into a rising political star". In 1892 he became Gladstone's Home Secretary, and in 1908 Prime Minister. It was also in 1892 that he met his second wife, the "sparkling and waspish" Margot.

Across the road, two blue plaques on **No.20** salute the Freud family, Sigmund and Anna. This is now the Freud Museum and a Listed building. The Austrian father of psychoanalysis, the 'Copernicus of the Mind', moved here with his daughter Anna from Elsworthy Road in September 1938 (see p 37), and died here a year later. The Museum, which was opened in 1986, four years after Anna's death, reflects the life and work of father and daughter, including his collection of antiquities and much of their furniture, especially The Couch. In 1952 Anna opened her Child Therapy Clinic here, which has now transferred to **Nos.12,14 & 21** under the title the Anna Freud Centre.

Behind a pleasant paved garden, **No.16A** was built in 1930 by Baron Arild Rosenkrantz and called The Little House, although it contains two ample studio flats. Rosenkrantz was a Danish stained glass artist, who designed windows for many English churches, such as St Paul's, Onslow Square. Further plaques appear on **No.6** and **No.4**, a black one on the former, to mark the birth in 1882 of Westfield College, and a blue one on the latter, recording the residence of Cecil Sharp, the folk song and dance man who died here in 1924. At the corner is the Roman Catholic **Church of St Thomas More**, which originated in the studio of No.3 Fitzjohn's Avenue in 1938 and moved to its present site in 1953: the new circular church, designed by Gerard Goalen, was built in 1967-69. Pastoral care was handed over in 2005 to the Opus Dei organisation, based at Netherhall House (see later).

Where the road bends to the left, **South Hampstead High School for Girls** was opened in 1882 by Princess Louise (see inscription). Established by the Girls' Public Day School Trust, it started life in Winchester Road six years earlier as the St John's Wood High School. The 'comely frontage' of the new school, designed by E C Robins, was commended by *The Builder*, which also noted that "the fives courts are not yet completed". During the last war, all the pupils were evacuated and some of the buildings were used as a fire station. The temporary firemen based here included Stephen Spender and William Sansom, and in 1942-44 Spender and his wife occupied a flat next door to the fire station. Since the war, the school has acquired several adjoining sites, including the home of Sir Ernest Waterlow RA, which the school demolished but commemorated in the blockish Waterlow building of 1988.

Walk back up to Nutley Terrace passing on the north-west corner **Netherhall House**, a residence for (mostly non-UK) graduate students (of any or no faith), owned by the Netherhall Educational Association and supervised by the Catholic organisation Opus Dei. Further up on the left, **No.43** has since the early 1960s housed the Danish YWCA. **Nos.51&53**, dating from 1938, sport a pair of fairly hefty nymphs on their frontages. The architect of **No.48**, a modernist house of 1939 with an odd pierced-metal balcony, was Herrey Zweigenthal.

Maresfield Gardens continues northwards, but we return to Nutley Terrace and walk to the T-junction with **NETHERHALL GARDENS**, also named after a Maryon Wilson property in Sussex. Starting out as Netherhall Terrace, the street was given its present name in 1877 and immediately attracted the nicest sort of resident. Some of the early houses have survived, including **No.6** (to the left, where the road bends and plunges down to the Finchley Road), now Frazer House, but originally called Culloden when built by Batterbury & Huxley in 1882 for the successful historical painter Thomas Davidson: initials and date are on the house, which has since 1954 been the British College of Osteopathic Medicine.

No.7 was for many years the home of Louis Sinclair MP (1861-1928), who according to *Who Was Who* profited so much from "commercial pursuits" in Australia that he retired from business at the age of 25. **No.5** and **No.12** are the junior branches of North Bridge House and South Hampstead High School respectively. A blue plaque on **No.10** (early purpose-built flats) records the first home of social reformers and historians Sidney and Beatrice Webb after their marriage in 1892. On the corner with Nutley Terrace, **No.14**, Otto Schiff House, which caters for senior Jewish citizens, bears its date (1885) and the initials of its first owner, John Carrington. On the opposite corner, the **Southbank International School** occupies **No.16**, a stylish reconstruction of the former red-brick edifice, built in the wake of a much contested redevelopment in the 1990s. The similar **No.18A** now houses the **Netherhall Educational Association** and **No.18B** the **Netherhall International College**.

Follow Netherhall Gardens northwards. **NETHERHALL WAY**, a no-through road to Frognal, was so named in 1942. It adjoins the home ground of (Sir) Stephen Spender, who grew up at No.10 Frognal. Netherhall Gardens, full of substantial if unremarkable houses, bends to the east (delightful modern Orchard Corner in the angle) to pass the top end of Maresfield Gardens and reach Fitzjohn's Avenue. **No. 51** on the left has a blue plaque to John Passmore Edwards, who lived here from 1908 until his death in 1911. He is described as "Journalist, Editor and Builder of Free Public Libraries", but he spent much of his publisher's profits on hospitals and horse troughs. There is no plaque on the attractive **No.59**, where the Irish tenor, Count John McCormack, lived during WWI. Crossing the road, note **No.70 Maresfield Gardens**, which was mysteriously called The Wong in the 1920s, when it was the home of solicitor Sir Arthur Johnson, first Town Clerk of the Borough of Hampstead and also its first Freeman.

Further up Netherhall Gardens on the right, examine a black plaque for Sir Edward Elgar on the gatepost of **No.42**. The famous architect Norman Shaw built a house for Edwin Long RA on this site in 1888, and it was occupied by the composer with his family during 1912-21, renaming it Severn House to show his Worcestershire connections. He chose this mansion with its art gallery and billiard room to demonstrate that composers in general, and he in particular, could live in the grand manner.

Severn House was his status symbol, but it also nearly broke him, and he admitted later that he had to accept commissions for trifling theatrical works in order to keep the house up. It was later demolished and replaced in the 1930s.

We reach **FITZJOHN'S AVENUE** again. On the corner **No.61**, a Listed building of 1878, was the first of two houses built near here by Norman Shaw for the now forgotten Edwin Long RA. The DNB says he "excelled as a painter of oriental scenes", but an anonymous contemporary claimed that "Art is long but Long is not art". The curious architecture with Dutch gables and large bow window is commended by Cherry & Pevsner. Walk further up the hill, keeping on the left-hand pavement. Novelist Stella Gibbons had a bed-sitter at **No.67** in 1930-32, during the time she was giving birth to her classic *Cold Comfort Farm*. Parts were also written on the Northern Line, she says, en route to offices of *The Lady* where she then worked. **No.69**, described by Pevsner as "polychrome Rundbogenstil", is now **Devonshire House School**. There are currently six schools in Fitzjohn's Avenue, which helps to explain the morning and tea-time traffic jams. (The upper part of Fitzjohn's Avenue is surveyed in *The Streets of Hampstead*.)

Cross the avenue with care to the higher of two narrow passages, **SPRING PATH** and **SHEPHERD'S PATH**, which preserve old field paths, deriving their names from Shepherd's Well (p 56), and walk down the hill. The rebuilding of **No.80 FITZJOHN'S AVENUE**, formerly well known locally for the notes of music on its wrought-iron fence, caused local uproar in 1988, when developers who had permission for 'partial demolition' demolished everything except for one chimney stack; the music faded away too. The new house has an attractive octagonal tower and tries to get on with its neighbours. Much further down the Avenue, **Nos.58-64** enjoy friezes of encaustic tiles, while **Nos.54-56**, dated 1878, are two of several houses here with floral eaves and decorated roofscapes. No.56 was in the 1880s the home of Sir Max Pemberton, author of *The Diary of a Scoundrel* and other novels.

We, however, turn left and take the right-hand fork past the ivy-covered arms inviting visitors to **No.1 AKENSIDE ROAD**, built in 1889. The road is named after a curious character, Mark Akenside, who frequented Hampstead Wells in the middle of the 18th century. The son of a butcher from Newcastle, Akenside had medical ambitions, but he failed to become a successful Hampstead doctor because of his poetic hauteur. Hampstead air, he said, was "fatal to nothing except the prosperity of physicians". However, he later became chief physician of St Thomas's Hospital and also achieved fame as a poet. "A tame genius", said Horace Walpole. Akenside Road closely follows an old track, seen on Rocque's map of 1745, connecting Belsize with the pure water of Shepherd's Well. The street was first laid out and named in 1878, but No.1 is the only house in the road listed in the 1890 Directory. A recent addition is **Copperbeech Close**, down the hill on the right, where the houses are close but the tree is missing.

Well before Copperbeeh Close comes the entrance to a curiously shaped 'Gothic' house, actually **No.33 DALEHAM GARDENS**, occupied in Edwardian times by Colonel Arthur Barham, son of Sir George Barham, a Mayor of Hampstead (p 27). Now named **Gloucester House**, it is owned by the Tavistock and Portman NHS Trust and includes the Mulberry Bush Day Unit and the Monroe Young Family Centre. The latter was previously called the Marilyn Monroe Centre, because profits from a book about this luminary were offered to the Unit. It seems that this corner of Belsize can now treat problems, both physical and mental, from cradle to the grave. Across the road **No.32**, also with entrance in Akenside Road, is a charming coach house with hoist, cupola and weathervane, initialled B; this was the stabling of No.33, and like the latter bears a terracotta stork, part of the Barham crest.

We turn right into Daleham Gardens, named after a 15th-century house on the Maryon Wilson's Sussex estate, not far from the villages of Maresfield and Nutley. The southern stretch of Daleham Gardens was fully developed by 1885 by H & E Kelly, who also built much of Fitzjohn's Avenue. On the way down the hill we pass the eastern end of **NUTLEY TERRACE**, which was originally called Nutley Gardens. Before WWII, **No.4** was the Nutley School of Languages and after the war resounded to the combined typewriters of novelist Gavin Lyall and journalist Katharine Whitehorn. When **Nutley Cottage,** to be glimpsed near the centre of this eastern stretch, came on the market in 1987, the estate agents claimed that this bijou residence had been built in the 1860s, graced by the presence of Lillie Langtry, and used as Edward VII's billiard hall. None of these facts could be confirmed, though there is evidence to suggest that this was once the billiard room of No.44 Fitzjohn's Avenue.

On the corner, **No.31A DALEHAM GARDENS** is a recently built neat block of Old People's Housing. Further down, **No.22** was during the 1930s a boarding house run largely for Jewish refugees by Sybil Knight; she and her family often appeared in famous pictures made by one of her lodgers, noted German photographer Bill Brandt. **No.17** was a hostel for unmarried mothers in the 1950s, but is now the Leo Baeck Day Centre for the Over Sixties. The title commemorates the theologian who became president of the Institute of Jews from Germany, and is a reminder that Hampstead was a popular refuge for many Jews escaping from Nazi oppression in the 1930s. Most of the houses at the lower end share an ornate style, with oriel windows and a flourish of fruit and flowers moulded in the plastered gable ends (pargetting), some daringly picked out in colour. At the bottom, bordering

21 The former *Three Gables*, Fitzjohn's Avenue (Norman Shaw, 1881)

Belsize Lane, **No.1** is the headquarters of various psychological organisations including the C G Jung Clinic. The Institute of Group Analysis is the main training centre for group therapists in the UK. More physical help is available at **No.5**, the **Daleham Gardens Health Centre**. Across the road, **No.6** has a date plaque of 1883 and a Latin tag offering "Either Peace or War". This was presumably the family motto of the first resident, Andrew Donaldson RA, painter of historical and religious pictures, who died here in 1898 and whose initials are still visible.

DALEHAM MEWS, embarking on an attractive curvaceous career opposite the end of Nutley Terrace, was developed at the same time as the Gardens, primarily to provide stabling for the local residents, and later to hire, sell or service other forms of transport. John Fernald, theatre director and lecturer, inhabited the vine-clad **No. 2** from the 1950s until his death in 1985. His recreations, according to *Who's Who*, included "producing Tchekov and looking at cats". The actor, Roy Kinnear, lived at **No.33** in the 1960s. Properties on the east side of the Mews line the boundary of the old Maryon Wilson estate.

The bottom of the Mews emerges into the ancient thoroughfare **BELSIZE LANE** (pp 46-49). Turn to the right but look across the road at the Listed buildings **Nos.79-93** which form an attractive terrace, each house with balconies and (stone) roses round their rounded doorways. They are the original Belsize Terrace referred to as new houses in the Vestry Minutes of 1856 (see map p 25). Further on, **No.101** is a picturesque, converted coach house, complete with weathercock. On the corner of Daleham Gardens is **Daleham House**, part of the Tavistock's Mental Health and Social Care department and immediately after it the **Tavistock Centre**, more popularly known as the **Tavistock Clinic**, which we glimpsed shortly after embarking on this walk (p 57). This was established in 1920 in Malet Place (near Tavistock Square) by doctors experienced in treating shell-shock in WWI. Now famous for its more general psychotherapeutic work, the Clinic moved in 1967 to its present bulky building, designed by F. Maunder. After the mission hall on this site (**[19]**, p 57) had been demolished, a grand house called Three Gables arose here **[21]**; it was designed by Norman Shaw in 1881 for Frank Holl, a fashionable portrait painter. In the 1930s it was replaced by a Marie Curie Hospital, bombed in WWII.

A left turn at the Freud statue at the corner of Fitzjohn's Avenue brings us back to the starting point of this walk, near the Swiss Cottage Underground station and bus stops.

Route 8

The Lyndhurst area

Circular walk from St Stephen's

For map see p 64

North of Belsize Village, a group of roads curiously carry the names of Lord Chancellors of the Georgian era, including Lords Thurlow, Eldon and Lyndhurst, who never lived in Hampstead. But Alexander Wedderburn, who became the Earl of Rosslyn, certainly did, and it was he who started the fashion for these lordly street names.

Born in Edinburgh in 1733, Wedderburn moved to this area from Branch Hill Lodge (see *The Streets of Hampstead*) in 1794, having acquired the leasehold of The Grove House: this mansion dating back to the 16th century stood between the top of the present Lyndhurst Road and Wedderburn Road. As Lord Loughborough, he had also acquired the reputation of being 'a second Judge Jeffreys' for his harsh treatment of the Gordon Rioters in 1780. His Hampstead residence, which he renamed Shelford Lodge, was his country retreat. (One of his town houses was No.6 Bedford Square, which ironically bears a plaque to his great rival, Lord Eldon.) Here, says his biographer, "by sobriety, regularity and temperance, he prolonged a feeble existence". By 1802 he was too feeble to maintain 21 acres in Hampstead, and

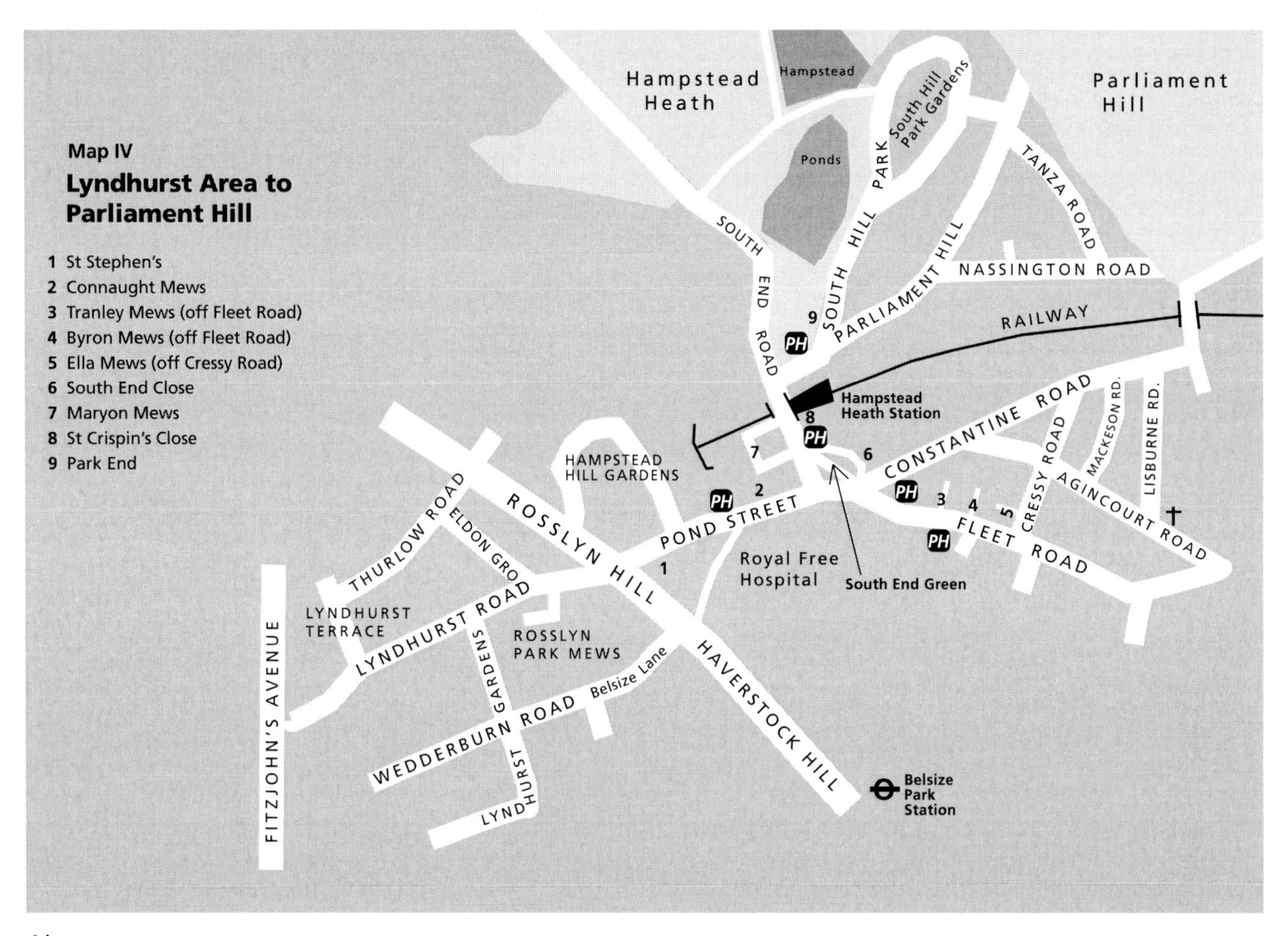
Map IV
Lyndhurst Area to Parliament Hill
1 St Stephen's
2 Connaught Mews
3 Tranley Mews (off Fleet Road)
4 Byron Mews (off Fleet Road)
5 Ella Mews (off Cressy Road)
6 South End Close
7 Maryon Mews
8 St Crispin's Close
9 Park End
Hampstead Heath
Hampstead
Ponds
South Hill Park Gardens
Parliament Hill
SOUTH END ROAD
SOUTH HILL PARK
PARLIAMENT HILL
TANZA ROAD
NASSINGTON ROAD
RAILWAY
Hampstead Heath Station
CONSTANTINE ROAD
MACKESON RD.
LISBURNE RD.
CRESSY ROAD
AGINCOURT ROAD
FLEET ROAD
South End Green
Royal Free Hospital
POND STREET
HAMPSTEAD HILL GARDENS
ROSSLYN HILL
HAVERSTOCK HILL
THURLOW ROAD
ELDON GRO
LYNDHURST TERRACE
LYNDHURST ROAD
ROSSLYN PARK MEWS
LYNDHURST GARDENS
Belsize Lane
WEDDERBURN ROAD
LYNDHURST
FITZJOHN'S AVENUE
Belsize Park Station

retired to Slough, where he died three years later. His Hampstead mansion was quickly renamed Rosslyn House **[22]**, probably by a later occupant, Robert Milligan, projector of the West India Docks, which Wedderburn had strongly supported. A more recent Earl of Rosslyn achieved fame as the model of 'the Man who broke the Bank at Monte Carlo'. The Rosslyn name, derived from the Roslin estate (famous for its chapel) near Edinburgh, lives on in Hampstead streets and shops, and in a Roehampton Rugger Club which began life in Pond Street.

Other occupants of Rosslyn House included (Sir) Francis Freeling, Secretary to the General Post Office, and Henry Davidson, a West India merchant, who began developing the property as the Rosslyn Park Estate in the 1850s. The house had also been considered by Queen Victoria as a nursery for the royal children. In 1855, after a major rebuild, Rosslyn House became an emergency shelter for seventy girls orphaned by the Crimean War. The Soldiers' Infant Home, which later became the Royal Soldiers' Daughters Home and School, originally trained its charges for domestic service. By 1858, the charity had found better premises at Vane House in Rosslyn Hill, and Prince Albert came in person to lead the girls up the hill to their new home. The last owner of Rosslyn House was Charles Woodd, a wine merchant (see p 13 for further Woodds), who bought it in 1859 and whose widow sold it to developers in 1896, with its "handsome wrought iron gates and a splendid avenue of sycamores".

Start across the road from St Stephen's, this time on the corner with **LYNDHURST ROAD**, whose lower stretch here follows the line of the ancient Rosslyn Grove that led from the main road to the gate of Rosslyn House. Once called the Chestnut Walk, the

22 Rosslyn House, demolished 1896

avenue was notable not for sycamores but for Spanish chestnuts, and by the late 18th century had become mostly a public thoroughfare. Rosslyn Grove was still used as an address in Edwardian times. Above the entrance to Rosslyn House, Lyndhurst Road was laid out and developed by Henry Davidson in the early 1860s. Many of the houses were built by Thomas Clowser of Hampstead High Street. Lord Lyndhurst was John Singleton Copley, son of the painter of the same name, and was Lord Chancellor three times between 1827 and 1846: he is buried in Highgate Cemetery.

Prominent at the corner where you are standing is the former Congregational Church **Lyndhurst Hall**, which was built in 1884 in the front garden of what is now No.11 Rosslyn Hill. The massive hexagonal church of purple Luton bricks was designed by Alfred Waterhouse, also responsible for the Natural History Museum, the original University College Hospital in Gower Street and other important buildings, and is thought by many a pundit to be one of his best works. The first minister was the dynamic Robert F Horton, 'the Billy Graham of his time', who stayed for nearly 50 years. The church closed in 1978 and has been converted into a state-of-the-art recording studio complex. This is Air Studios, where many recent film and rock-and-pop albums have been recorded. The original architect is honoured in the adjoining **Waterhouse Close**, Council housing for the elderly, built in 1978 in the back garden of Rosslyn Lodge.

The Lodge has been subsumed into the **Olave Centre**, named after Lady Baden-Powell, which is the headquarters of the World Association of Girl Guides and Girl Scouts. There was a house on this site from the mid-18th century, and from the 1780s it was used by the Nihell family as a boarding school and a Catholic chapel (this was before St Mary's, Holly Place, was opened). Rosslyn Lodge was built about 1803 by Henry Cooke, a merchant from Highgate then living in Rosslyn House. From the 1830s it was the home of (Sir) Arthur Blackwood, who later became Secretary to the Post Office (as did, coincidentally, his near neighbours Rowland Hill and Francis Freeling), and from 1848-56 of Count Edward Zohrab, a Turkish diplomat. During WWI the Lodge was used as a military hospital where over 2000 patients were treated. "It is noteworthy", said the *Hampstead Advertiser* after the war, "that no deaths occurred". Later the building became a hotel, a hostel, and a nurses' home, until it was bought by the Girl Guides in 1982 and tactfully restored by John Dangerfield Associates. A plaque over the front door helpfully gives a potted history of the house, which has sprouted an annexe, called Pax Lodge. Another plaque of 1989 commemorates World Chief Guide Olave Baden-Powell.

Uphill from the Olave Centre, **ROSSLYN PARK MEWS** originated in 1866 but was rebuilt in 1967-68. Beyond the Mews, **Nos.12-18 LYNDHURST ROAD** were erected in 1870-71 (No.13 shows its date, 1871, in curiously deformed characters). No.12 was the home for many years of Dr Stanley Sadie (1930-2005), the distinguished editor of Grove's Dictionary of Music from 1970 onwards. Note the bell-pulls on No.18.

The ball-topped pillar at No.18 and the gatehouse across Lyndhurst Gardens at No.19 are relics of a grand entrance to Rosslyn House created by Charles Woodd in the 1860s. The gatehouse **[23]** was designed by the great S S Teulon, then engaged in building St Stephen's, of which Woodd was a generous benefactor. But the pillar is not where it was (it has been moved several feet), and the gatehouse is not what it was. According to the late Roy Allen, who researched this area thoroughly, "Teulon's gatehouse projected into the present thoroughfare, towards No.18, and therefore gave a somewhat narrow entrance to Lyndhurst Gardens when that street was started in 1882. On the demolition of Rosslyn House in 1896, the authorities insisted on widening the road. Horace Field (another Hampstead architect), who had done work for Woodd and was now engaged on **Nos.19-21** Lyndhurst Road, something of Teulon's work and gave his client in No.19 an interesting coach-house." The front of the building bears the Woodd coat of arms, which can also be seen on the Woodd tomb in the parish churchyard.

23 Gateway to Rosslyn House, 1860s version. A ball-topped pillar and part of Teulon's gatehouse have survived.

came up with a rescue plan. The structure was sliced through on the desired line, and a new outer wall was built, using original materials; into this were inserted a large window and the 1865 date stone from the demolished part. Field thus preserved Field's three handsome houses are now Listed. Lord Cottesloe, chairman of many enterprises, notably the National Theatre, lived at No.21 in the 1970s.

Look across the road at the top of the attractive **Coach House, No.11B,** built by Henry Davidson in the early 1860s to house the coach of No.11 Lyndhurst Road, while his **Landau House, No.11A,** accommodated the landau of No.1 Eldon Grove. Landau House was the home of the eminent art historian Professor Lee Johnson, an expert on the painter Delacroix, until his death here in 2006.

No.22, which was built about 1896 for Russell Rea MP, is currently being revamped and extended, in the same "flashy" style remarked upon by Andrew Saint. **Nos.23-26** are of the same period by W A Burr.

On the north side of Lyndhurst Road **Nos.1-11**, first known as Rosslyn Bank, were built by Henry Davidson from 1863. We approach from No.11. The landscape artist Carl Haag (a favourite of Queen Victoria) claimed that his house (**No.7**) was similar in design to the Red Tower at Oberwesel on the Rhine. Another resident was the actor Richard Burton, remembered for rehearsing Shakespeare on the lawn of **No.6** during his Old Vic season in the early 1950s. **No.5** was designed by A W S Cross, and **No.3** was one of the local homes of architect Henry Spalding (Spalding & Cross built the Liberal Club at 24 Heath Street).

Lyndhurst Road originally terminated at No.31 on the south side and on the north at Lyndhurst Terrace (along the boundary of the Rosslyn House estate), hence the idiosyncratic numbering we have encountered. But in 1883 the road was extended to Akenside Road, and thus into Maryon-Wilson land and the burgeoning boulevard of Fitzjohn's Avenue.

Turn right into **LYNDHURST TERRACE**, which was also built by Davidson in the first half of the 1860s and called variously Rosslyn Park or Windsor Terrace. The latter name was chosen because Windsor Castle was visible from here across the undeveloped acres of the Conduit Fields. The present name came into force in 1939.

The turreted Gothic villas **Nos.1-3** (Listed II*) have had a complex history of being separate but linked, then being united but later divided. **Old Conduit House**, referring to nearby Shepherd's Well, is now the name of No.1, originally Bayford House, and **Hall Place** is No.3, first called Oswald House. They were built in 1864 by Charles Buckeridge for two brothers-in-law, both stained-glass artists: Alfred Bell, co-founder of Clayton & Bell, and John Burlison, co-founder of Burlison & Grylls. Bell gave the parish church most of its present windows.

Another attractive house opposite, **No.2** (**The Hermitage**), was built in 1862 with ornamental verandah and brickwork for George Dighton, "a painter of much promise and a distinguished rifle shot", said Henry Crabb Robinson. **No.5** was the stables for **No.7** (Springmead), which bears a roundel containing an owl and "Nil sine labore". This was doubtless the motto of (Sir) Hugo Hirst, who lived here from 1899 and was the hard-working chairman of the General Electric Company. The modern block **Newmount** is on the site of New Mount Lodge, built by one Joseph Neuberg and, evidently at the suggestion of his friend Thomas Carlyle, named after himself (a literal translation from the German). **No.15** was for many years the home of Baroness Serota of Hampstead, who had a distinguished political career; she died here in 2002. The substantial **Elm Bank**, now **Nos.17** and **19**, was the first house in the street to be occupied. Julian Layton, who lived here until his death in 1989, was a wealthy stockbroker, who helped thousands of Jews to flee Nazi Germany.

Also developed by Davidson in the early 1860s, **THURLOW ROAD** was named after the first Baron Thurlow (1731-1806), an eminent lawyer with a reputation as a sound constitutionalist. After becoming Lord Chancellor for the second time, he presided at the trial of Warren Hastings, but after intriguing with George, Prince of Wales, against Pitt was forced to resign in 1792. Thurlow often visited Romney at his studio in Holly Hill. Most of the original, stuccoed Italianate houses in the road have survived, and some have stunning front gardens. **No.1** has retained its separate bells for Visitors and Servants. Among long-term residents in the road have been the writer Paul Bloomfield, who died at **No.2** in 1987, and the artist Mary Hill, famous for her postcard views of Hampstead, who lived at **No.8**. In the same house (from 1954) lived the Bulgarian author Elias Canetti, who won the Nobel Prize for Literature in 1981. He wrote a sensational memoir of his Hampstead days, *Party in the Blitz* (2005), which included his assignations with the then unknown author Iris Murdoch – at No.8. At the end of the 19th century, **No.12** and **No.26** housed the popular girls' school Tremarth, which later moved to Prince Arthur Road, only to be demolished in 1935 and replaced by the apartment block Greenhill.

The circle of D H Lawrence descended on **No.28** on Thursdays during 1918-22, when the Hon. Dorothy Brett (usually just 'Brett') held her salons here. The bohemian daughter of Viscount Esher, she was an artist and a confidante of Katherine Mansfield, who nonetheless called her "a rotten, mushy kind of female". When Middleton Murry became too familiar with No.28, Katherine mocked Brett's "dirty neck and film on teeth" and asked "is there no tap at Thurlow Road that she can put her toothbrush under?" Virginia Woolf sampled the salon and was equally catty, but the artist Mark Gertler liked it so much he became Brett's lodger.

The first occupant of **No.30** was its architect, Horace Field, whose eponymous son was born here and became an even more successful 'arts and crafts' architect. Lloyds Bank on Rosslyn Hill is his major local work, but his transformation of No.30's dining room makes an impressive illustration in Thompson's history of Hampstead.

ELDON GROVE is named after the Georgian Lord Chancellor, John Scott (1751-1836), who became Lord Eldon. He was the popular successor to Rosslyn when the latter was dismissed from the woolsack in 1801. This street was also laid out in the 1860s, and was known as Eldon Road until the 1930s. (The old name is still visible on the side of No.29 Thurlow Road.) Davidson had difficulty in finding builders to develop this road, as much of it was over a newly-dug tunnel of the Hampstead Junction Railway. Eventually in 1864 he built a pair of houses himself, **Nos.4&5**.

Charles Knight, the publisher, lived at **No.7** from 1864 to 1870. Dedicated to popular education, he was responsible, with his friend Sir Rowland Hill, for founding the Society for the Diffusion of Useful Knowledge, and as the editor of the *Penny Magazine* he aimed to demonstrate that, even if something was cheap, it could also be of good quality. In the 1920s **No.8** was the home of the Blackett family, of whom (Baron) Patrick won the Nobel Prize for Physics in 1948 for his discoveries in the field of cosmic radiation. The first house (No.1) to be built in the road was Eldon House, on the site of **Tower Close**. The painter William Dobson RA, who specialised in scriptural subjects, lived here from 1860 until 1883, and was followed five years later by the talented Allingham couple. William, the poet and friend of poets, who died at Eldon House in 1889, is mainly remembered now for *Up the airy mountain, down the rushy glen*. His wife Helen was a much-loved water colourist whose country scenes, especially with thatched cottages, have recently become very popular: she is well represented and documented at the Hampstead Museum, Burgh House. Eldon House was demolished in 1973 and ten years later came Tower Close, "of stunning external appearance, with a definite mediaeval accent", said one critic, and "a rare example of the zanier levels of Post-Modernism", said another (Alan Powers). It was developed and designed by Pollard, Thomas and Edwards. A new **Eldon House** round the corner was also their work.

Nos.14-16 were not built until 1911. Dr Richard Barnett, the archaeologist (he excavated Nineveh *inter alia*) lived at No.14, until his death in 1986. The eminent drama critic and writer J C Trewin lived for many years at **No.15** and died there in 1990. His wife Wendy was also a noted drama critic. From 1936 to 1939, **No.3** was the home of the painter Paul Nash. Among his subjects he used a grotto in his garden here, which was in fact the grave of a previous owner's dog.

In 1880 the Willetts announced their 'Belsize Court Estate, South Hampstead'. This was mainly **LYNDHURST GARDENS**, but it included three houses at the top of Belsize Crescent and livery stables in Belsize Lane. Belsize Court, which had shed most of its 16-acre grounds for the Willetts' development, was an impressive house **[24]** to the north of the present eastern stretch of Wedderburn Road. Built in 1811 by George Todd on the site of a previous dwelling known in 1714 as the White House, the mansion was called Bellesize Villa (1840), Belsize House (by 1855, when the original of that name had been demolished), and eventually Belsize Court (1874).

The most notable occupant, from 1833 to 1869, was Matthew Forster, city merchant, ship owner, and MP for Berwick-on-Tweed from 1841 to 1853, when he was unseated by a bribery scandal. He was a close friend of the poet Letitia Elizabeth Landon, better known as L E L, and notorious for her liaisons with literary lions. She stayed at Belsize Court en route to the Gold Coast in 1838, where she died of an overdose of drugs. Forster also contributed to the abolition of the West African slave trade by importing palm oil from the area (for lubricating railway axles), which African chiefs found more profitable than selling slaves.

The last inhabitants of Belsize Court were members of the Bergheim family, whose history has recently been researched by Mary Shenai and published by the local Conservation Area Advisory Committee. John Bergheim was an oil magnate from

24 Belsize Court, a 19th-century view from the south (as it were, from present Wedderburn Road)

Turkey, who leased Belsize Court in 1898 and was notable for his musical parties: these often featured the young pianist Artur Rubinstein, whom the Bergheims had befriended and helped to promote.

The old Belsize Court is remembered as a white house with a five-barred gate across its entrance in Belsize Lane (just before the Lane bends sharply to the south). A few old trees from its garden still flourish, including

a large one which was on the boundary line of the Belsize Court garden at the present junction of Lyndhurst Gardens and Wedderburn Road. The property was sold by the Church Commissioners in 1937 to John Laing, who erected the five low-rise blocks of flats named **Belsize Court**.

All the original houses in **LYNDHURST GARDENS**, with one exception, were by the Willetts' architect Harry Measures. "A cracking series of Queen Anne villas", says Andrew Saint, "crow-stepping, soaring chimneys, terracotta details, cut-brick ornament, Measures gives you the lot." There is a particularly striking group (all Listed) on the north-east side, the dragon-topped **No.26** being the Maria Montessori Training Organisation, and **No.24** the Lyndhurst House Preparatory School.

Opposite is the only non-Willett house, **No.17**, The Hoo. This corner of the estate projected into the grounds of Rosslyn House, and it seems that Woodd, alarmed at the height of the new houses, bought the plot from the Willetts in 1889 and got Horace Field to produce something more discreet; and very pleasant it is, with its tile-hung south front and large hooded porch. Says Alastair Service in his *Victorian and Edwardian Hampstead*: "This is one of the best pieces of architecture in Hampstead", but since 2002 the building has been much converted to the needs of various units of the Royal Free and, latterly, the Social Care Trust.

At the junction with Wedderburn Road, the pillar box is of the 'anonymous' type of 1883-87: the words 'Post Office' and the Royal Cipher had been forgotten. This was put right with the next batch, as may be seen in Lyndhurst Road.

Beyond the crossroads and further down on the right lies **Edenhall**, the admirable Marie Curie Hospice, which includes a day-care centre for cancer patients. Further south, at least three houses had a lightning conductor adorned with a sunflower, but this feature survives only at **No.14**. Round the corner are some more Willett houses. During WWI, the prettily-porched **No.4** became the Artists Rifles VAD Hospital.

After a slow start, Lyndhurst Gardens seems to have gone fairly well for the Willetts. Sixteen of their villas had been sold by 1890. But then taste turned against these tall, labour-intensive basement houses, and the remaining four were slow to sell.

The old (western) part of **WEDDERBURN ROAD** came from the grounds of Rosslyn House, and was started by Charles Woodd in 1884, but in his lifetime the only development was on the south side, well away from the house. Here the attractive designs were by Horace Field, including Wedderburn House (**No.1**), probably the first mansion block in Hampstead, ready by October 1885. Among the early occupants were two Misses Field, maiden aunts of the architect. **No.3** and **No.5**, showing Field's homely features, such as small-paned windows, date from about 1886, while **No.7** and **No.9**, in very different style, followed a few years later. **No.11** and **No.13** with Dutch gables are "more showy" (Pevsner). No.13 was leased in WWII by Anna Freud as her War Nurseries for war orphans and children who had lost their homes in the Blitz. Profiting from her experiences here, she later developed her famous clinic in Maresfield Gardens (p 59). In the 1980s, **No.15**, once owned by comedian Peter Sellers, was briefly occupied by the comedian Marty Feldman. Across the road, **No.18** was for many years the home of British chess champion Richard Griffith.

The north side of the road was started in 1895, after Woodd's death, but before Rosslyn House came down. The architect was W A Burr, who also did good work in Bracknell Gardens. A notable resident at **No.4** was the Dame Edna from down under, Barry Humphries. Next door are two distinctive, attractive "pastiche modernist" apartment blocks called **Andrew Court**.

Across the road the space left by the demolition of No.13 Lyndhurst Gardens was partly filled in 2004 by another apartment block, **Burlington House**: the surrounding garden was fought for and won by the local residents' association.

From here, a short walk eastwards will bring you back to Rosslyn Hill and bus services to north and south.

Route 9

Pond Street and the Fleet Road area

Sinuous walk ending at South End Green

For map see p 64

Start at the corner of **POND STREET** and Rosslyn Hill, on the corner by mighty St Stephen's (p 10). Pond Street is certainly one of the oldest streets in Hampstead, and probably the oldest street name. Amongst several early references there is one in 1607 to an application for a 'licence to enclose a parcel of the waste soil lying between Pondebrooke and Donningtons

at the lower part of Pond Street'. There is also a record of some victims of the Great Plague having lived here.

By the early 19th century, the pond **[25]** that was connected to the brook, one of the headwaters of the River Fleet, had become so muddy and isolated that it was first fenced and then filled in, about 1835. Until the late 1840s the name Pond Street applied not only to the road, but to the whole South End Green area. This was a hamlet of its own, until the development of the Downshire Hill area in Regency times drew it into the town. Around 1800, Pond Street accommodated so many doctors it was known as the Harley Street of Hampstead. Among those present were Baron Dimsdale, who had inoculated against smallpox the Empress Catherine of Russia, and Dr Thomas Goodwin, who discovered some local 'Neutral Saline Springs' and promoted yet another Spa.

Take the first left turn and walk to the far end of **HAMPSTEAD HILL GARDENS**, which was developed on land belonging to George Crispin: it had been seriously considered by the Vestry as a site for their new town hall. The earliest houses, all stucco villas, were erected by 1870 at the Pond Street end, but it is the later red-brick, Queen Anne style houses at the other end enjoying the curve of the road

25 South End Green
from the bottom of Pond Street, c.1830

which are the main attraction. These were the jewels in the crown of Batterbury & Huxley (p 9) who built them, mainly for prosperous artists, between 1875 and 1881. With their ornamental friezes, moulded swags and other decorations, the houses have been much praised by the experts. (Sir) John Summerson, who lived in **No.14** in the 1930s, noted they were "all bedecked with the neatest rubbed-brick ornaments and reminiscent of the houses which occur in Kate Greenaway drawings". The two houses at the western approach stand as gatehouses for the entrance, though the southern one is numbered in Rosslyn Hill. **Nos. 16** and **20** were early addresses of St Christopher's School, now in Belsize Lane. Aldous and Maria Huxley lived at **No.18** in 1919-20, their first married home.

Walk back towards Pond Street. Nos.1-11 and No.2 are Listed. **No.11** displays its date (1881), its original name, Aspens, and the initials of its first owner, Charles Gurden. **Nos.5** and **7** are dated 1879, as is **No. 9**, built for the watercolourist Thomas Collier. A recent resident here was the architect Norman Foster (supporting the theory that modern architects live in old houses). **No.5** has a fine wrought-iron gate, with initials JR. The CG on the plaque of **No.3**, 'built AD 1877', stood for Charles Green, the successful illustrator of Dickens and many periodicals. **No.1** was the first headquarters and exhibition centre of the Hampstead Artists Council and, from 1946 until his death in 1984, the home of the poet Sir William Empson (see also p 15) and of his flamboyant wife Hetta, the 'sculptor and socialite'. On the other side, **No.2** has a weatherboarded coach house (No.2½) and a fine wrought-iron gate, showing its date 1888 and initials GB: this was installed by George Bell, the publisher, who lived here from 1882 to 1890.

Back in **POND STREET**, look across at **Hampstead Hill School** in the old church hall of St Stephen's Church. The foundation stone of the hall notes that it was built in 1908 and designed by E A Pearce: its bellcote gives it a nice villagey look. Substantial **Nos.1&3** on your right, and on your left **Nos.5-13**, were all built (and numbered) as part of Hampstead Hill Gardens in the late 1860s. They are notable for the bearded heads on their fascias (lost from No.5): the houses are now Listed. The 1885 Directory shows James Brumbridge, cowkeeper and dairyman, at No.11, then No.47 Hampstead Hill Gardens. An arched entry leads to a converted coach house, **No. 13A** (the number writ large in roof tiles). **No.15**, the **Roebuck** tavern and hotel, displays a fine polychrome buck in its pediment.

Across the way, the unmissable **Royal Free Hospital** dominates the skyline. The Free Hospital was founded by William Marsden in Hatton Garden in 1828, and revolutionised health care by offering free treatment to all. It was given the title

'Royal' by Queen Victoria in 1838, moved to Gray's Inn Road in 1840 and graduated to Pond Street in 1974, bringing with it its wrought-iron tympanum of 1894 (displayed outside). The Royal Free took over from the Hampstead General Hospital (p 11) and the North West London Fever Hospital (p 11) and now has some 900 beds and 4500 staff. The curvaceous sculpture on the forecourt is by Jesse Watkins (1974). The hospital was officially opened by Elizabeth II in 1978, 150 years after the hospital's birth. The architects were Watkins, Gray, Woodgate International.

Nos.17-21 date from the late 18th century, according to the DOE Listing. Several of these houses have narrow frontages but considerable depth, for example No.17, where the artist and critic Richard Carline lived from the 1930s to 1982. Under an arch, a passage leads to **Connaught Mews**, recently redeveloped. **Nos.23-25** were built around 1900 as the headquarters of the First Cadet Battalion of the Royal Fusiliers. Their drill hall was also used from 1908 by Hampstead's first Boy Scouts troop, founded in the year of Baden-Powell's clarion call, and claiming to be the oldest troop in existence. Though now a social services office, No. 23's castellation shows its connections with the adjoining hall. The Armoury Health Club was for many years called the Harben Armoury after Hampstead's first mayor, Sir Henry Harben (p 43). The **Staff Day Nursery** next door, founded in 1906, was rebuilt in 1928 and reopened by Princess Mary. Note the commemorative roundel, also the cherub in the pediment.

An ancient holly tree hides the front door of **No. 31**, which was built in 1832. This was the home of Sir Julian Huxley, biologist and first director-general of UNESCO, who lived here from 1943 until his death in 1975 (see plaque). His wife Juliette, sculptor and writer, died here in 1994. **Nos.33** and **35** are Listed as early 18th century; the latter, probably of 1730, has handsome cherubs and rams' heads. The studio at **No.35A** was built by the graphic designer F H K Henrion, who lived here from 1946 until his death in 1990. A pioneer in the field of corporate design, Henrion was responsible for the logo and lettering of, among many others, the National Theatre, the Post Office and British Airways. The studio is now the Hampstead Clinic of Chinese Medicine.

At the foot of Pond Street is **Warwick Mansions**, where George Orwell lodged in the 1930s. He is commemorated in a plaque (restored in 2001), which includes a portrait of the author, on **No.1 SOUTH END ROAD** at the corner. Once a pie shop and dairy, this property became Albert Ward's art gallery in 1900. In 1934 this was Book Lovers' Corner, and the young Orwell came to work here as a part-time shop assistant, living at the proprietor's flat in Warwick Mansions next door. Local scenes were reflected, not very favourably, in his novel *Keep the Aspidistra Flying*, published in 1936. (South End Green has also featured in Le Carré's *Smiley's People* and Wyndham's *Day of the Triffids*.) From the 1960s these premises housed a café called The Prompt Corner, which later became a pizza parlour, then a burger bar and is now a café again.

The greening of **SOUTH END GREEN** began with the filling in of the main pond in 1835, but the name first appears on Cruchley's map of 1847. Originally part of the Pond Street colony, and only approached by that roadway, the Green was opened out by the building of South End Road in Regency times, the coming of the railway in 1860 and the laying out of the Fleet and Constantine Roads in the 1870s and 1880s. The land was bought by the Vestry from the Lord of the Manor in 1874, and soon became a major traffic centre, which it has remained. A swathe was cut through the green in 1886 for the London Street Tramways Company and, at the time of Bank Holiday fairs, trams would arrive at the rate of one a minute.

In 1910 a local commentator noted that the only green left in South End Green was the paint on the railings round the fountain. This public **fountain** was presented in 1880 by Miss Anne Crump of Hereford House (on the south side of the Green) to refresh the many Heath visitors and "to help stop intemperance and vice". Designed by J H Evins in pure Early English, it offered "accommodation for 16 persons and 4 dogs". The comedian George Grossmith (of Haverstock Hill) was among those at the official opening and recalled that his first stage performance (as Hamlet) was at Hereford House. The fountain had to be moved in 1886 to allow room for the trams, and had to be restored and reopened in 1974 after many years of drought. The ceremony was performed by Sir Julian Huxley. After further periods of drought and vandalism, the fountain was reopened in 1993 by Michael Foot, and again in 2006 (without water) and 2007 (with water). The area around the (Listed) fountain has recently been given shrubs and lawns and the paving stones have been engraved with quotations from local literati, ranging from Keats to Agatha Christie. This is now a welcome oasis of sanity amid the mad traffic centre of South End Green.

Hereford House was pulled down in 1913 to be succeeded by the Hampstead Picture Playhouse, which became the Classic and then Cannon cinema – and finally the ABC, which closed in 2000. The site is now filled by a **Marks & Spencer** food store and a large **Panoramic** block of apartments.

Across the road are the **public lavatories** with their fine wrought-iron work. They were built in 1897 as a convenience for passengers at the tram terminus, and were Listed in 1993 as one of the few remaining Victorian lavatories in London. In 1987 they were featured in the film about Joe Orton *Prick Up Your Ears*.

Turn right down **FLEET ROAD**, on the line of an ancient footpath alongside the Fleet River linking South End Green with Gospel Oak. When Mr Lund was developing his St John's Park Estate (p 9) to the south in the 1860s, he considered the Fleet area to be too low-lying, ill-drained and unhealthy to be fit for middle-class housing. Instead, he planned a series of terraced houses and shops, with mews and stabling attached. There had already been problems with the Pond Street sewer (which benefited only the local watercress beds), and with the Midland Railway's new tunnel. Then in 1870 a smallpox epidemic caused a fever hospital to be hastily assembled near Lawn Road, with patients being brought in by wagon. Property values plummeted, and Lund barricaded off Fleet Road to divert the wagons through Haverstock Hill. In 1872 fever sufferers were replaced by mental cases, but 4 years later the fever patients were back and the 'temporary' hospital became permanent. Notwithstanding the high boundary wall built round the hospital grounds, the area's reputation was ruined, and Fleet Road remained a demarcation line between dignified Belsize Park to the south and the "lower end of middle-class respectability" to the north. To the dust and thudding of a Carpet Beating Ground was added in 1887 the rattle and rumbling of trams, for which a local depot was built. Many tram workers settled in the neighbourhood.

On the corner of Fleet Road and the Green, **The White Horse** stands on the site of other pubs of that name dating back to at least 1721. The present version was designed in 1904 (see plaque) by Albert Pridmore. An appeal was launched in 1998 to preserve the pub's clock, which George Orwell mentioned in *Keep the Aspidistra Flying*. On the other side of the junction, a British Legion Hall (1924-45) has been replaced by the Panoramic flats and other enterprises. To the south is a clutter of buildings, mostly of Royal Free appendices. Another pub, **The Stag** (1869) at the corner with Lawn Road was called the Stag & Abigail in the 1921 Directory (but as the landlord's wife was called Abigail, this may be a misdirection). A rather battered plaque in the wall beside it refers to the boundary line of the North Western Fever Hospital. Next to **No.144, Tranley Mews** is the new name of the area that housed the Fleet Laundry for many years. Next to **No.136** is another (gated) residential development, **Byron Mews**. Because of planning blight, Mr Salter was still working his brickfields here until the Vestry called a halt in 1885. In 1891, the Census taker recorded Henry Hall, a travelling showman, living in a caravan on the site of the future **No.106** (currently a fish and chip shop).

Beyond Cressy Road, on the left, is the main entrance (masked by a fence and hedge) to the **Fleet Road Primary School**, which was opened by the School Board for London in 1880. It was so successful under the inspired leadership of Henry Adams and his wife that people claimed that it took children "from gutter to

26 Fleet Road School, c.1907, cookery class

university" and was "the Harrow of the Board Schools" **[26]**. Between 1958 and 1961 it was amalgamated with Haverstock School, Chalk Farm, when part of the site was vacated to allow for the construction of the present school, opened in 1969. The blocks of flats on the opposite, south side, above Upper Park Road, replaced war-damaged terraces in 1963. Designed by E F Jacob, Hampstead Borough Architect, they are named after three notable Hampstead residents, Sir Francis Palgrave, Sarah Siddons and Robert Stephenson. The 1850s curved terrace on the left, running from **No.32** to **No.4**, was restored and converted by architects Anthony Richardson, and earned them an RIBA Community Architecture award in 1990-91. **Nos. 28-32** are called Robert Grace House after their young architect who died in 1986. **No.6** was Moll's Bakery from 1929 to 1981. **No.4** was for many years an oil merchant's, with three large coloured oil jars on its façade. These were taken down by Camden Council and put into storage. The passage next to No.4 follows the line of the historic boundary between Hampstead and St Pancras. Across the road we see **No.19, Chapel Studios** (**[27]**, p 77), built in 1878 as St Saviour's Mission and School. It was here that Charles Mackeson, the future first Vicar of All Hallows, Gospel Oak, began his ministry. Later it became the Wharrie Hall, named after Sir Henry Harben's married daughter (see also p 12). A frequent user of these studios was film director Anthony Minghella. Next door at **No.17**, the South Hampstead Working Men's Club is recorded in 1885. This later became the Parkhill Chapel, and now functions as **The Beacon**. All these building developments took place before Mr Lund's barrier at Lawn Road was removed by the Hampstead Vestry in 1881.

Cross **AGINCOURT ROAD** at the lights and turn left into it. The names Agincourt and Cressy Road (p 78) both presumably refer to English victories against the French in the 15th century, though why they were chosen when the streets were laid out in 1878, and why Crecy is misspelt, remain a mystery – unless the latter name referred to the watercress beds of the River Fleet. First on the right is the entrance to a modern office development, **Heathgate Place**, which includes the headquarters of the Anthony Nolan (Bone Marrow) Trust. It abuts the yard in front of the **Gospel Oak Methodist Church**, whose address is in Agincourt Road although its entrance is in Lisburne Road, into which we now turn. This road was named (again inexplicably) in 1887; a Gospel Oak Methodist Chapel had been established here 5 years earlier. This building lies beyond the present Gospel Oak Methodist Church and is now used as a nursery school. One of the many foundation stones gives the architect as Charles Bell FRIBA, who also designed the circular wards of New End Hospital. The chapel was used as such until 1900, when it was succeeded by an octagonal *church* erected alongside, one of the last buildings to be made of the red bricks from Gospel Oak brickfields. This church had been elegantly designed by Professor Beresford Pike. A notable feature was a tower surmounted by a lantern and consequently dubbed 'The Lighthouse' (**[28]**, p 78). Unfortunately, an errant barrage balloon coiled its cable round the tower in WWII, and this led to the demise of both. The **present church** was built in 1971. A few green glazed bricks bought by chapel supporters for the 1900 building appeal can still be seen in the boundary wall hard up against Heathgate Place (formerly the interior of the church).

The houses in **LISBURNE ROAD** are on a smaller scale than their neighbours', but have a merry, bobbly skyline, as on the east side of Agincourt Road. This area's main developer, T E Gibb, being short of capital, considered erecting workmen's cottages in Lisburne Road, and even raised money by letting the site to Lord George Sanger's Circus for winter quarters, actions which incurred the wrath of Lord Mansfield, owner of the land nearby. A recent resident at **No.26** was Claudia Jones, a notable Civil Rights worker and founder of the *West Indian and Asian Gazette*. All the streets in this neighbourhood were included in the Mansfield Conservation Area in 1990. "The individual buildings are not that amazing," its chairman said, 'but it's the overall pattern that's important. We're half trying to preserve what is here and half trying to make it better."

27 Chapel Studios, Fleet Road, built (by Batterbury & Huxley) as St Saviour's Mission Room, 1878

Lisburne Road leads into Constantine Road (see below). Turn left, and left again, and traverse **MACKESON ROAD**, built 1887, which was named after the Reverend

28 Photograph of the 1900 Gospel Oak Methodist Church: tower feature on the left; on the right, a caretaker's creeper-covered cottage on what became the entrance to Heathgate Place

Charles Mackeson, founder of All Hallows in Savernake Road. The development here was originally defined as "lower middle class rather than upper working class". Apart from the bombing in-fill at **Nos.23-29**, the houses have kept their period flavour. **Nos.11-21** on the right have noticeably grander doorways. **Nos.1-9** and **2-12** have some good gauged-brick mullions.

Mackeson Road leads back into Agincourt Road opposite a blank red-brick wall. To the left of this is the original Fleet Road Infants' School, which was vacated in 1969 and became **Agincourt House,** an Education Centre. Notice the original railings beside it and the playground of the primary school beyond. We, however, turn right and, at the next corner, left into **CRESSY ROAD** (the name is discussed on p 77). In the middle is a striking **ambulance station** (1975). Designed by the Architects' Department of the Greater London Council in the 'hard red brick' style made famous by James Stirling in the 1960s, it supplanted the previous station situated behind the Stag. Previously on this site was a factory dubbed 'The Mill' by its founders Mansell, Hunt and Catty, who in 1883 started to make "articles in paper for the serving of food and decoration of the table". They became a major local employer, expanding into a second large building, 'The Office', across the road, where now stands the Camden Council IT Department, recently named **The Roy Shaw Centre** (see plaque) as a tribute to that distinguished and long-serving Councillor. An adjoining office development is called **ELLA MEWS**. The doily and cracker factory remained in business until 1969. Residents remember the factory hooter at 8:30 am, lunchtime 2 pm and finally at 6 pm, and the wire pulley system for exchanging messages across the road. Beyond the ambulance station used to be the Cressy Works Piano Factory of Messrs Wheeler and Strickland, opened in 1892, at **Nos.2-4**; No.2 is now a hostel for the single homeless.

Turn back along Cressy Road and pursue it to **CONSTANTINE ROAD** (1887), another inexplicable name, where we turn left. Tramway history was made here in 1901, when the loop line was created to avoid trams backing down Fleet Road. It was one of the first examples of one-way-street working, and the last stretch of tramway built for horse trams. Horses gave way to electricity in 1909. The LCC's trams continued running to South End Green until 1938, when trolley buses took over: these lasted until 1961. The petrol-driven No.24 bus began its historic route in 1910. Walk along the left-hand pavement (odd-numbered houses) between the pleasant, unremarkable terraces to the fork where Agincourt Road leads off to the left. Facing the fork, unique **Sunnyside** has a château-style roof with fish-scale slates. It was built for himself by Robert Thorpe, who helped to develop this area. It has no street number. Cross here to **No.38** and note that **Nos.38-24** have mostly kept their stained glass and, up in the gables, their anonymous escutcheons. **No.30** had its troubles in 1908, when Dr Hawley Crippen installed his mistress, Ethel le Neve, here. From this house the couple fled after the doctor had murdered his wife in Hilldrop Crescent. (Or did he? The case has recently been reopened.)

The visionary artist Albert Houthuesen (1903-79) grew up at **No.20** and attended Fleet Road School. The poverty-stricken family moved from Amsterdam to Constantine Road (first to **No.7** and later to No.20, virtually opposite) in 1912, after his mother had lost control, according to Houthuesen's obituary, and "struck her husband on the head with a shoe – a blow from which he died." The artist, who remembered his life in Hampstead as one of penny-pinching and pawnshops, did not receive recognition until after an exhibition in 1961, followed by an appearance on television: four of his works are in Tate Britain. **No.18** has a clock mosaic on its doorstep (sometimes covered with a mat) showing the time of 12:20, the exact moment that Queen Elizabeth II was crowned. The houses on the north side as we approach South End Green are numbered **1-5 Elm Terrace**, after Elm Tree Cottage previously on the site.

At the terminus for buses (formerly for trams) at South End Green, look right. **South End Close,** four handsomely designed blocks of LCC flats, were erected in 1920. These are on the site of Pickett's farm (also known as South End Farm, and earlier, Holylands, named after its farmer), and on a piece of waste land used for some of Hampstead's earliest fairs. Semi-permanent swing-boats, and eventually steam roundabouts, were set up by the Gray family, who later moved to the Vale of Health. The flats displaced an all-purpose rubbish dump, know by the locals as 'the Little Place'. The foundation stone on Block A, rather shrouded in shrubs, gives the architect as C Wontner Smith.

From here you can either continue on Route 10 or take one of the several buses which depart from the South End Green terminus or the bottom of Pond Street, outside Marks and Spencers.

Route 10

From South End Green to Parliament Hill

Circular walk from South End Green

For map see p 64

To the north of **SOUTH END GREEN**, on the eastern side of the road lies the mock-Tudor tavern **The Garden Gate**, formerly The Railway Tavern, on the site of an ancient beer-house called The Perseverance. The old railway coalyard next to it was transformed in 1984 into a modern leafy estate. Thirty-six houses were built on this 'seemingly unpromising site' and given a seemingly inappropriate name, **St Crispin's Close**. Asked to explain, the developer claimed only that 'it sounded a nice name', but its relevance is remarkable for its proximity to Crispin's field (see p 73) and Agincourt Road (see *Henry V*).

Hampstead Heath Station was opened in 1860 on the Hampstead Junction Railway (later North London Line). It immediately attracted hordes of East Enders intent on enjoying their 'Appy 'Ampstead, especially the Bank Holiday fairs on the Heath. The original station was the scene of a disaster at Easter 1892, when a sudden heavy shower drove large crowds from the fair into the building. As Barratt recorded, "immense numbers pressed forward to the staircase leading to the up platform and, being unable to force a passage because of a ticket collector's box at the bottom, were thrown into such confusion that it was impossible for all to extricate themselves." Eight people were crushed to death and many injured. The present low-profile station, after suffering years of Silverlink, is now part of London Overground: this was launched here by the Mayor of London (see plaque) in November 2007. (South End Road north of the station is covered in *The Streets of Hampstead.*)

The widening of the **rail bridge** (completed 1969) prompted local protest at a possible four-lane Hampstead by-pass, taking in some of the Heath, and gave birth to the South End Green Association, which has thrived ever since. A plaque on the bridge notes that it replaced a 20-ft wide cast-iron bridge built in 1864. In 1978 local enterprise also took over and restored the **allotments** along the railway, which are much in demand: they are run by the South End Green and Mansfield Associations.

Almost opposite, between shops, is **MARYON MEWS**, named after a nearby Maryon House, which disappeared in the late 18th century. (The Maryons were Lords of the Manor of Hampstead.) A block of stables and a timber-curing shed have also gone. An attractive new mews of 24 houses was ingeniously squeezed into the hinterland in 1975, designed by Ted Levy Benjamin & Partners. (This is now a gated no-go area.)

Beyond Hampstead Heath Station, the Parliament Hill and South Hill Park area was cut off from the rest of the Belsize estate by the Hampstead Junction Railway (the earliest name of the line here) in 1860. This sliced right through the 50 acres of Pickett's Farm. The three remaining fields were developed from the 1870s, partly by Thomas Rhodes of St Pancras, and partly by the farmer himself, Joseph Pickett.

Turn right into **SOUTH HILL PARK**, which was laid out in tennis racket shape to make best use of the space available. The first building in the street was **The Magdala,** a pub that was already there by 1868. It was named after a bitter battle fought that year in Abyssinia, where the self-styled Emperor Theodore III had imprisoned all European residents and their consuls. A British expeditionary force under General Napier had to storm the heights of Magdala before final victory. There is now a tiled painting of stormy heights (signed Stirling 98) in the entrance. It was outside this tavern in 1955 that Ruth Ellis waited for and shot her lover, afterwards being the last woman ever to be hanged in Britain. The incident was dramatised in the 1985 film *Dance with a Stranger.* By a macabre coincidence, the second to last woman to hang, Styllon Christofi, lived in the same street and committed murder here also in the mid-1950s.

Opposite the tavern, a small piece of wooded waste ground has been earmarked by Camden for a World Peace Garden.

The road bends to the left going up the hill; walk up the right-hand side admiring the substantial Victorian houses, still in good shape, for example **Nos.1-3**, formerly part of the Hampstead Home Hospital (p 81). Between Nos.15 and 17, look across the road at a glimpse of trees on Hampstead Heath and the top of the spire of Christ Church. **Nos.29** and **31** are bombing replacements, built in 1962 and 1959 respectively by two different but harmonious architects, T G Ingersoll and Michael Brawne. Pevsner commends No.29's playful polygonal bay. **No.39** was the home of Joan Robinson, creator of the *Teddy Robinson* stories for children, until her death in 1988. The road forks here; continue on the right-hand pavement. **Nos.51-55** form an idiosyncratic terrace with ogival centre steps and unusual ornamentation spread over the central doorway.

The houses across the street are Nos.1-23 **SOUTH HILL PARK GARDENS**. This was the last group of houses to be built in this area, probably an unpleasant surprise to the original occupants of South Hill Park, who expected real gardens in the centre of the tennis racket. Most of the houses are substantial, double-fronted and well-kept. Many façades have keystones and capitals with faces of cherubs or ferns. Pevsner liked the modern **No.7, Oliver Court,** as "a neat demonstration of cross-wall construction". From the

1930s the successful commercial artist Vernon Ward lived at **No.8**. He was born over his father's art gallery and antique shop on South End Green, and died in South Hill Park Gardens in 1985.

Continue up **SOUTH HILL PARK. No.57** was briefly the home of Andrew Fisher, who rose from pitboy to be thrice Prime Minister of Australia: he died here in 1928 and was buried in Fortune Green Cemetery. Ignoring the tempting passageway inviting you to go through to Parliament Hill, continue to **No. 85**, the house Joseph Pickett built for himself and where he stayed until his death in 1893, and to **No. 93** near the top of the hill, the home of guitarist John Williams in the 1970s. The next houses after this, **Nos.95-107**, have rewarding views of Hampstead Heath, as do those which follow – now numbered evenly, from **No.118** downwards, on the north-western edge of the tennis racket. Between **Nos. 96** and **94** is a charming view down the paved path to one of the Hampstead Ponds. Filling a bombing gap are two modern developments, **Nos.80-90** (by and for Bill Howell and Stanley Amis, 1953-6) which "have a reticent, well-proportioned street frontage", according to Pevsner, who by contrast calls **No.78** (by and for Brian Housden in the 1960s) "a strange Brutalist composition of concrete and glass." The old No.86 was the house where Maxim Litvinoff, the Bolshevik refugee and Lenin's man in London, lodged with his recently married wife, Ivy Low. It was here in 1917 that he learned of the Russian revolution and, "seething with excitement", as he wrote in his journal, "I tried to shave with the toothpaste and got into the bath without turning on the tap". He later became Russia's leading foreign commissar.

No.66 was for many years the home of artist and teacher Klaus Meyer, who died here in 2002, and of his wife Celia, a popular nursery school head. Next to **No.58**, suitably called Buena Vista, is a splendid narrow view across the Heath to the Christ Church spire. A recent resident at **No.26** was writer/director Anthony Minghella, who died here in 2008. Many of the houses in this part of the street have delightful decorated porches: some have coats of arms and others have bulls' heads. Below No.16 is **PARK END**, once a hive of small industries and now the home of an eponymous GP surgery: this enclave was built on part of the lowest Hampstead pond, which was filled in at Mr Pickett's instigation in 1892.

Now turn up **PARLIAMENT HILL** past the sturdy Council block **Parliament Court**. Parliament Hill is named after the nearby eminence on Hampstead Heath, which indisputably allows a fine prospect of the Houses of Parliament. Quite untrue is the local legend that Guy Fawkes's fellow conspirators assembled here on 5 November 1605, in the hope of witnessing the Westminster explosion. (The Plot was actually discovered the day before, and on the 5th the conspirators would have been fleeing for their lives.) Others claim that the name derives from the folk moots or parliaments held here long before Westminster was born. Joseph Pickett began building here over his old farmland in 1880, helped at first by the Kentish Town builder John Ashwell.

Among the earliest arrivals were **Nos. 1-3** on the left, built for the Hampstead Home Hospital, which rapidly expanded into South Hill Park and in 1904 transmogrified into the Hampstead General Hospital bordering Hampstead Green. Most of the original houses have survived, of which good representatives are **Nos.32-38** and the houses opposite, **Nos.37-43**, with their stained glass and decorative bargeboards. Several artists resided in this road. Maeve de Markievicz, who lived at **No. 30** after WWII, was notable not only for her painting but for her mother, Irish-born Countess Markievicz. She was sentenced to death after the Easter Rising of 1916, but survived to become the first woman elected to the House of Commons. Being a Sinn Feiner, however, she never took her seat. Harold Gilman, a leading artist in the Camden Town Group, came to **No. 33** in 1917, but died here two years later during the great influenza epidemic. **No.57** was the home of Tom O'Brien, eminent trade unionist, until his death in 1970. From 1919 to 1958 Harold Brighouse, author of the popular play *Hobson's Choice*, lived at **No. 67**.

No.68 was the final home of the poet Anna Wickham, who moved from Downshire Hill in 1919. Famous for her artistic salons, which included D H Lawrence, Edith Sitwell and many impecunious writers, she also gave shelter to Dylan Thomas. During one long visit, Thomas wrote *Adventures in the Skin Trade* in the bathroom here, accompanied by Anna's caged canaries. Appropriately in 1984, a further plaque was awarded to George Orwell on **No.77**, where the writer lodged for barely six months in 1935. He was still working at the bookshop on South End Green (p 74), and still writing *Keep the Aspidistra Flying*, but wanted to live near the Heath. His months at No.77 were amongst his happiest, as here he met his first wife, Eileen O'Shaughnessy, whom he married the next year.

The road ends abruptly where Parliament Hill Fields begin, and where the old boundary between the parishes of St Pancras and St John at Hampstead is marked by a sign

St P P M | St J H

low down on the brick pillar. Here, Pickett had expected to link up with developments on Lord Mansfield's estate. Fortunately, the Fields were bought for the public in 1889, and Pickett had to console himself by building **TANZA ROAD** instead. This leads off between Nos.58 and 62 Parliament Hill. Before "Tanza" was agreed in 1894, the name was spelt Tanser and may derive from Tansor, a village in Northamptonshire. (But why?) Early residents objected to a name that sounded like a German dancer and asked in vain for something "more in keeping with the character of the Freeholders". The gardens of the red-brick, 4-storey semi-detached houses on the north-east side run along the old boundary between boroughs (see above). **Nos.33-35** show a date plaque of 1890. Richard Garnett, Keeper of Printed Books at the British Museum, lived at **No.27** until his death in 1906 (see Garnett Road). Another literary scholar (a Dickens expert), Professor Kathleen Tillotson, lived for many years at **No.23** and died here in 2001.

Tanza Road leads into **NASSINGTON ROAD**, now delightfully lined with silver birch trees, which was laid out in 1878 and probably also named after a village in Northamptonshire a few miles from Tansor. As with the adjoining roads, the mainly semi-detached houses, designed for middle-class occupants, were "respectable but not expensive". At the end leading directly to Parliament Hill Fields, **No.26** was the home (1934-9) of Wilfrid Gibson, profilic poet and self-styled "spokesman for the inarticulate poor". The path from here to Highgate was once the only permitted route across the Mansfield estate; the only people who were allowed on the grass, where cattle safely grazed, were chimney sweeps, who took carpets to beat there in summer.

Many houses in this and neighbouring roads sport fine bargeboard decoration at the gable ends – sadly shaved off in some cases, perhaps at a time when such Victorian frolics were out of favour. Other period details, such as stained glass, tiled paths and glazed doors, can be enjoyed at **Nos.13-17** and **47-53**. The artist Alan Adams, who lived at **No.43**, held an exhibition at Burgh House in 1983, when he was 90, and one of his ceramic sculptures is on permanent display there; he died in 1988.

Up the hill on the right-hand side, a roadway between Nos.6 and 4 leads to "**1-6 THE OLD ORCHARD NW3**", a 1970s development of two terraces of three delightful small houses designed by Trevor & Beaven, constructed despite local residents' fruitless campaign to preserve the original orchard.

Regain South End Green, from where a variety of buses can take you in a variety of directions.

Sources

Books

Baines, F E. *Records of the Manor, Parish and Borough of Hampstead.* Whitaker/Hewetson, 1890

Barratt, Thomas J. *Annals of Hampstead.* Black 1912, Leventhal 1972

Bebbington, Gillian. *London street names.* Batsford, 1987

Cherry, Bridget & Pevsner, Nikolaus. *The buildings of England. London 4: North.* Penguin, 1998

Cohn, Leonie (ed.). *Belsize Park, a living suburb.* Belsize Park Conservation Area Committee, 1986

Howitt, William. *The Northern Heights of London.* Longmans, 1869

Jenkins, Simon. *Companion Guide to Outer London* (Collins, 1981)

Jenkins, Simon and Ditchburn, Jonathan. *Images of Hampstead.* Ackerman, 1982

Maxwell, Anna. *Hampstead.* James Clark & Co., 1912

Norrie, Ian and Mavis (ed.). *The Book of Hampstead.* High Hill Press, 1968

Oppé, E F. *Hampstead – a London Town.* The author, 1951

Oxford Dictionary of National Biography (abbreviated as *DNB*). OUP, 2004

Park, J J. *The topography and natural history of Hampstead.* Nichols, Son & Bentley, 1814, 1818

Pevsner, Nikolaus. *The buildings of England – London II.* Penguin, 1952

Richardson, John. *Hampstead One Thousand.* Historical Publications, 1985

Service, Alastair. *Victorian and Edwardian Hampstead.* Historical Publications, 1989

Shenai, Mary. *Finding the Bergheims of Belsize Court.* Belsize Conservation Area Advisory Committee, 2007

Shire, Adrian (ed.). *Belsize 2000, a living suburb.* Belsize Conservation Area Advisory Committee, 2000

Summerson, John. *Georgian London.* Pleiades, 1945

Thompson, F M L. *Hampstead, Building a Borough 1650-1954.* Routledge & Kegan Paul, 1974

Victoria History of the County of Middlesex, Vol IX. OUP, 1989

Walford, Edward. *Old and new London*, Vol V. Cassell etc, c.1880

White, Caroline. *Sweet Hampstead and its associations.* Elliot, Stock, 1900

Maps of Hampstead

Rocque 1746; Goodwin/Neele 1803; Park/Newton 1814; Ordnance Survey 1822; Cruchley 1829; Weller 1862; Daw 1864; Ordnance Survey 1866, 1895 and later

Other sources

The Hampstead & Highgate Express

Camden New Journal

Camden Local Studies and Archives Centre

LCC Street Lists and GLC Street Naming section

Greater London Record Office

The Victorian Society's Hampstead Walks, by Andrew Saint and David Prout

The Camden Society of Architects' Walks

Guildhall Library

Librarian, Eton College

Camden History Reviews

Street Directories, Rate books, Census returns

Church and School Histories

Department of Environment (DoE) Lists

Dictionaries of British Artists (Johnson & Creutzner; Waters & Wood)

Newsletters of local organisations:

Friends of Belsize Library, Belsize Residents Association, Friends of Hampstead Town Hall, South End Green Association

Index

Streets included in the survey are indicated in boldface, as are the main entries for these and other selected subjects;
*** = illustration**
PH = public house

D

E

F

T